THE SHY-MAN SYNDROME

THE
SHY-MAN
SYNDROME

*Why Men Become Love Shy
And How They Can Overcome It*

DR. BRIAN G. GILMARTIN

MADISON BOOKS
Lanham • New York • London

4501 Forbes Boulevard, Suite 200
Lanham, Maryland 20706
UPA Acquisitions Department (301) 459-3366

10 Thornbury Road
Plymouth PL6 7PP
United Kingdom

Library of Congress Cataloging-in-Publication Data
ISBN: 978-1-56833-269-7 (cloth: alk. paper)

For My Favorite French-Speaking Gemini—
Coreen Sharon, of Upper Hutt, New Zealand

Contents

Foreword

If Shys Anonymous were to have a motto, it should be: "It takes one to know one." Only a *shy* knows the agony, torture and loneliness of how it is to have the shyness streak. Shys have an uncanny knack of knowing more about what other people are thinking than any other people on earth, including psychologists, social workers, psychotherapists and psychiatrists, of which I am one.

Dr. Gilmartin and I, as shys, came together in an effort to start a national Shys Anonymous—a would-be Sisyphean endeavor, for shys are so prone to remaining anonymous that to join Shys Anonymous is for them a gargantuan task requiring a Herculean effort.

Selling snow to Eskimos and sunshine to Floridians is easier than getting a shy to talk, relate, trust, give, yield, relax and be intimate. Balancing the National Budget is easier than the task of getting a shy to stop making excuses for his or her "perceived" inadequacies. Shys are a difficult bunch, and only someone with the patience of Job could wait for a shy to make a decision.

I speak of "perceived" inadequacies—That is exactly the correct word to use for how shys feel about themselves. They perceive they have great inadequacies and insecurities; and yet, most are very secure people. What paralyzes them is a *Behavior Inhibition Gene,* of which Dr. Gilmartin speaks.

The grand accomplishment that Dr. Gilmartin achieves in his book is to show that shys do have a way out of the shyness swamp and morass in which they struggle through life. Dr. Gilmartin, a shy guy himself, grabs the shy by the hand and as a big brother, leads interference at bulldozing down the papier mache monsters that plague the shy person as he or she fights to survive in a seemingly social world of happy, self-confident, "party" people. Dr. Gilmartin's mission is to tear down those mythical monsters of (1) self-consciousness in social situations; (2) fears of sexual inferiority; (3) preoccupations with fantasy hero-grandstanding; and (4) worry over sexual and social awkwardness.

Love-shyness is a plague to the male who ogles a girl and hopes to be the Prince Charming in her life. Guys who are paralyzed by the thought of being rejected by a girl may go through a whole lifetime of never kissing or coming close to making a date.

We often see on the walls of quaint Italian restaurants the saying, "A day without wine is like a day without sunshine." For the shy, that quote goes, "A day as a shy is a day with no fun, no joy, no nothing." Shyness is forever, but you can get control over shyness. Dr. Gilmartin describes, teaches and opens doors for shy gals and guys.

Dr. Gilmartin offers hope for that little orphan boy who thinks he'll never break out of his bubble. My son, Robert, a paralyzed shy for 19 of his 23 years, has himself emerged. With some heavy-duty advice from Dr. Gilmartin and his book, *Shyness and Love,* some crunching from me, and some "bite the bullet" sexual situations, Rob (as he is known to his girlfriends) made it out of Swamp Shyness. It was done by "doing what you don't want to do, and not doing what you do want to do"-type of behavior modification.

The turning point came in February 1988, when Dr. Gilmartin, Donna (my wife), and Robert met in Pigeon Forge, Tennessee, to start working on Shys Anonymous. Dr. Gilmartin's jolting, book-borne "fastballs" made Robert think twice about the life of the love-shy. After reading the book and surviving some tough group therapy skull sessions, Robert was a believer, and started to break some personal paralyzing taboos, and came bounding out of his shell. I, a sceptic—as are all shys—will bet on Dr. Gilmartin's zingers as being the answer to how to break the love-shy paralysis. It worked for Robert; I believe it can work for many more.

My hat is off to Brian Gilmartin. He knows more about shyness than anyone I have met; and knowing Brian Gilmartin—him knowing me—me knowing Robert—Robert knowing Brian—Brian knowing Robert, confirms the adage "It takes one to know one."

E. Michael Gutman, M.D.
President
Florida Psychological Society, 1988-89
Chief Psychiatrist
Mental Health Services, Orange County, Florida

Chapter 1

The Problem of Love-Shyness

During the last two decades, a great deal has been written about the so-called sexual revolution, but virtually no attention has been accorded a class of people whom the sexual revolution has bypassed: the "love-shy."

These are fully-grown men in their late 30s and 40s who are still virgins and who have less experience in dating, courting, and elementary kissing than the typical teenager. The love-shy also include 19 to 24 year-olds who shrink from the opposite sex in spite of strong desires for a close, loving heterosexual relationship.

These men are not homosexuals. They have heterosexual urges. They would like nothing better than to marry and have children but are prevented by severe shyness and social timidity.

Love-shyness is a life-crippling condition. Studies show that 85 percent of our greatest rewards in life derive from associations with friends, lovers, and family. Because of severe shyness and social timidity, the love-shy do not have friends, lovers, or family apart from their own mother and father.

Until quite recently a sizable proportion of the population, 1.7 million American males, has been almost totally ignored. Only last year was the first book on love-shyness published by the University

Press of America. The book you are now reading, a popular version, does far more than address the problem of love-shyness. It includes results of interviews with 300 love-shy men, ranging in age from 19 to 50. Their lifestyles, personal histories and thought processes were carefully scrutinized and compared to those of 200 non-shy men. In addition, various therapeutic and preventive approaches for dealing with love-shyness are reviewed. Those that have shown the greatest promise will be highlighted. Now, even the most severely love-shy man can be cured, comparatively painlessly, although the process requires time and resources, which are not available in all communities.

One of the major lessons I have learned from a decade of research on love-shyness is that the love-shy must band together both as a socio-political force to form groups such as *"Shys Anonymous," "Coed Scouts"* for shy, preadolescent children, and *"Practice Dating Therapy"* for teenagers and young adults. In that way, the love-shy can begin making themselves visible, their needs known and met.

Prevalence of Severe Love-Shyness

About 40 percent of all Americans suffer from strong feelings of shyness at one time or another. But only about 10 percent of all Americans suffer from endogenous or biologically-rooted shyness—a condition that scientists call behavioral inhibition. Another 10 percent are characterized by a high degree of biologically-based extroversion. These people are in need of almost constant excitement and stimulation.

Thus, only 25 percent of the 96.8 million Americans who label themselves as "shy" have endogenous or biologically-based inhibition/shyness. The remaining 75 percent suffer from exogenous or learned shyness, which cannot be explained by biologically-based or genetic factors. Those with exogenous shyness are normal in terms of native body biochemistry, neurology, brain biochemistry and physiology, genetics, etc.

They have learned to behave in certain ways when faced with stress in their environment. Thus, it is with "goings on" in the social environment that we must be concerned when we try to understand exogenous shyness. Labeled shy by parents, peers and teachers, impressionable children internalize and act out these labels.

Fortunately, there is strong evidence that virtually all cases of exogenous shyness can be cured by means of the various conventional approaches to counseling and psychotherapy. The 10 percent of the population with endogenous behavioral inhibition up to now has generally been quite refractory to therapy. Already genuinely inhibited due to body/brain biochemistry and neurology, these endogenous shys fully internalize their labels.

Despite these inborn disadvantages, most of them eventually marry. Because of good parenting and socialization practices even they can develop a reasonably effective set of social skills, interpersonal finesse, and social self-confidence.

My extensive work on severe and intractable love-shyness has convinced me that only about 1.5 percent of the population is so seriously disadvantagd that even normal patterns of dating, courtship and marriage are denied them. This 1.5 percent, the "love-shy," almost all males, are the subject of this book.

Just as 10 percent of all human males are born with endogenous behavioral inhibition, 10 percent of all females are similarly born with such biologically-rooted behavioral inhibition. But extremely few women ever find themselves inhibited from dating, courtship, or marriage. The reasons why will shortly become clear.

Of the approximately 5.5 percent of the male population in America that never marries, about half are believed to be homosexuals. About half of the remainder are heterosexuals who choose not to marry. The other half suffer from severe and intractable love-shyness. Milder cases of love-shyness also cause an enormous amount of emotional suffering and loneliness. According to syndicated advice columnist Ann Landers, the proportion of her letters containing complaints about shyness, about 10 percent, has increased noticeably over the past several years. The sexual revolution has provided those people no relief. In 1967, Stanford University professors Robert A. Ellis and W. Clayton Lane found that 25 percent of all university men surveyed were quite socially inactive because of shyness. They also found that eight percent of all heterosexual seniors had not yet had a date wth a girl.

A study published in 1973 by Judson T. Landis and Mary G. Landis further revealed that better than half of all college and university students experienced at least occasional severe shyness symptoms vis-a-vis the opposite sex in informal social situations. And 25 percent were victims of such severe shyness that they seldom or never dated. Only 23 percent were always or nearly always comfortable with opposite-sex age-mates.

The Gender Factor

Research clearly indicates that love-shyness impacts far more severely on males than on females. Women who remain without male companionship for long periods usually adapt well and often happily. For example, spinsters often become highly successful career women; they typically go through life with fewer mental and physical health problems than their married sisters. In stark contrast, the heterosexual bachelor has long been known to be vulnerable to quite serious and often bizarre pathologies.

Data recently obtained by Stanford University researcher Paul Pilkonis strongly suggests that shy women are no more likely to be neurotic than non-shy women. Shy men, on the other hand, are far more likely than non-shy men to suffer from severe neurotic conditions. Pilkonis also found that shy women were just as likely as non-shy women to enjoy close, same-sexed friendships. In contrast, shy men were far less likely than non-shy men to have any rewarding male friendships.

But Pilkonis' most important finding was that shy women were just as likely as non-shy women to date, to actively participate in the full range of courtship activities, and to marry. Shy men, however, participated far less than non-shy men in dating and in courtship activities. Many did not date at all. And shy men were far less likely than non-shy men to ever marry.

In American society, some shyness is tolerable and even socially acceptable in females. But in males of all ages, from kindergarten through adulthood, shyness is widely viewed as deviant and undesirable. Moreover, shyness in males inspires bullying, hazing, disparaging labeling and discrimination, whereas in females, shyness is seen as pleasantly feminine and nice.

In American society, it is the male who is expected to make the first move in romantic relationships, a requirement that has not been mitigated by the social changes of the women's liberation movement. In some areas, contemporary norms do allow women to initiate love-making. To be sure, contemporary norms permit a woman to initiate contact with a man after a relationship has already commenced, but they do not enable a woman to feel comfortable about asking a man for a *first* date.

Hence, shyness in women is very rarely found to be coterminous with love-shyness. In other words, extremely few shy women are also love-shy. Shy women are just as likely as non-shy women to date, to get married, and to have children. And they engage in these activities as early as do non-shy women.

Many studies have documented that men are far more susceptible than women to severe and intractable love-shyness. For example, in a 1983 study which incorporated a large sample of university students, sociologists David Knox and Kenneth Wilson found that 20 percent of the male students surveyed complained of painful feelings of shyness vis-a-vis the opposite sex in informal social situations, while fewer than 5 percent of the women students had a similar complaint. And very few of the women suffered emotionally from their shyness in the way men did.

A seldom-mentioned factor, which I believe increases the shyness (and diminishes the self-confidence/self-esteem) of young men as compared to that of young women, is women do the lion's share of the rejecting in male/female relationships. Within marriage, 90 percent of all divorces are sought by wives and not by husbands. And among courting couples at least two-thirds of all the break-ups are instigated by the female partner. In a well-known 1976 study by sociologists Charles Hill, Letitia Peplau, and Zick Rubin, girls terminated most of the "steady-dating" relationships.

Even normally self-confident men suffer more than women when relationships are terminated. Some victims of rejection become so emotionally scarred that they no longer can express their feelings even to themselves.

Even normally-adjusted young men experience significantly fewer serious man/woman relationships before marriage than even very average young women do. And I think this too bespeaks some of the serious shortcomings in contemporary courtship norms. Human beings do not like to be rejected. It can be extremely painful when a person is rejected by an opposite-sexed stranger upon asking for a date. And it can be profoundly devastating to the emotional well-being of a man when he is rejected by a woman with whom he had maintained a relationship over several months or longer.

Why does the American culture persist in requiring the male (not the female) to withstand the lion's share of such emotional devastation? I would suggest that the severe emotional scars and traumas endemic in severe and intractable love-shyness often reflect a history of rejection. In essence, if we are to move toward a fairer world, risk-taking involved in starting new relationships must be shared equally by women and men alike.

Inasmuch as love-shyness blocks and impedes men from living a normal life and does not do this for women, it is clear that love-shyness is a far more momentous problem for males than it is for females. Study after study have presented irrefutable evidence to the effect that men need women a great deal more than women need men. Women who for any reason remain in the single, never married category almost always manage to make an emotionally healthy adjustment. As we have seen, this most assuredly does not hold true for men.

Fear of the Informal

Social situations can be classified into two basic categories: (1) the impersonal, and (2) sociable or informal. Meeting potential dating partners/lovers can realistically only occur within the context of the second type of social situation, i.e., the informal, purely sociable situation. This is as true for meetings that occur in the workplace or at school, as it is for meetings that occur at parties. The workplace may be an impersonal setting, but a man must still find a way to bridge the gap between the impersonal and the personal/sociable.

Many social situations carry no clear script. As comedian Johnny Carson frequently points out, a person cannot enjoy full control in purely sociable, informal situations because he can never rehearse for his appearance.

Many people are also shy in certain kinds of impersonal social situations, and some are shy only in impersonal contexts. Impersonal situations likely to trigger shyness reactions include speechmaking, singing and acting in public, and piano playing. However, a curious truism is that many people who are severely shy in purely sociable situations are not at all uncomfortable in such impersonal, public performance situations. In fact, fully 30 percent of the chronically and severaly love-shy men who were studied for this book were not shy in impersonal social situations because they felt they were in control.

A person can go through life happily without getting over fears of public performance. But a person incapable of interacting in informal social situations cannot be happy or content. Shyness in social situations has a deleterious, damaging impact on a person's mental health, happiness and stability.

It is almost always easier to cure shyness in impersonal situations than in informal social situations. In order to function effectively in an impersonal situation, a person only needs to learn a "script" or "role" and gain sufficient self-confidence to go public with it.

On the other hand, in purely informal social situations there is no "script" or "role" to learn. Purely sociable situations are inherently ambiguous by nature. They require people to be themselves and improvise as they go along. In our highly competitive American society many people, especially males, do not really know who they actually are. People become themselves—develop a firm sense of identity—only through informal interaction from early childhood onward in friendship and kinship groups. For reasons this book will make clear, a significant minority of American boys grow up friendless, as social isolates.

Enlightened Self-Control versus Love-Shyness

Unfortunately, there are many influential people around who do not think love-shyness is a very important problem. In fact, some even view shyness as a blessing—a healthy yoke tying teenagers and young adults to the rigors of homework and study. Particularly in today's increasingly free sexual atmosphere, many parents and teachers wish love-shyness were commonplace.

What such parents and teachers fail to realize is that there is a big difference between enlightened self-discipline and love-shyness. The shy person cannot make choices. The shy person lacks the self-discipline and self-control necessary for commanding his performances in accordance with his own internalized values and wishes.

Love-Shyness Is a Serious Problem

One of the misconceptions people have about love-shyness is that it is "just a stage" through which many adolescents naturally pass. Unfortunately, the evidence strongly suggests that most love-shyness victims do not naturally outgrow the problem.

For most of its victims, love-shyness persists and profoundly affects their lives by preventing the development of good interpersonal skills crucial to career and personal success. And secondly, love-shyness prevents its victims from developing the netowrks of informal friendships, which are extremely important for the promotion of career effectiveness, community involvement, marriage-partner selection and even help in avoiding deviant or self-destructive behavior.

Dating Is Important

Going without female companionship is related to negative outcomes. For example, Harvard University sociologist Christopher Jencks followed a large sample of Indiana high school students for ten years until they were 28 years old. Among many other things, he compared men and women who had not dated at all while they were in high school with those who had dated. And his findings revealed that the non-daters were far less successful than the daters financially, in their careers, and in their overall adjustment. The more socially active a person had been during his/her high school years, the more successful and happy he/she was likely to be ten years later. Moreover, those young people who had been involved in steady dating relationships in high school tended to be best off ten years later in terms of economic and career success.

These findings were all much stronger for the men than they were for the women. The socially-active women were also better off ten years later than were the women who had been socially inactive while in high school. However, the differences between the socially active and inactive individuals were far greater for the males than for the females. In other words, the 28-year-old men who had not dated in high school were the least successful, happy and well adjusted.

The frequent dates had all been actively involved in same-sex peer networks, helping to build increasingly higher levels of interpersonal competence and social self-confidence. And interpersonal competence is the single, most important correlate of occupational and career success today. In fact, we are beginning to learn that interpersonal skills together with friendship networks represent the single, most effective ticket towards winning and keeping the best jobs. Dating also serves to build and enhance competitive effectiveness—another asset in the business world.

Studies in the Employment Sector

Social scientists have learned that better than 90 percent of all employment terminations from white-collar jobs are caused by deficits in interpersonal skills and not by technical shortcomings. In fact, among white-collar people who lose their jobs, only about one in 12 is terminated for reasons of technical incompetence. The other 11 are not regarded as good enough team players; they are not good at the small talk that prevails during coffee breaks and lunch hours. Supervisors and colleagues are uncomfortable with work mates who withdraw too much and are not relaxed or sociable.

Another little-known fact is that about 70 percent of the best job and career opportunities are obtained through informal social networks. Quite in spite of "Affirmative Action" and "Equal Opportunity Employment," only about 30 percent of the better job opportunities are obtained through such traditional sources as newspaper ads, personnel offices, employment agencies, etc. Moreover, recent studies show that jobs obtained through informal social networks pay significantly better, provide better growth opportunities, are about three times more likely to provide high levels of career satisfaction, and are about five times more likely to be retained by the incumbent for ten or more years.

Research also shows that among people of approximately the same education and technical training, employers are likely to prefer the warm, relaxed, naturally-sociable job applicant. The incumbent of any position who has an easy-going, natural command of strong interpersonal skills and finesse is the one who is likely to be promoted the fastest and least likely to be laid off when things get tough.

In addition, several studies show that deficits in actual job performance are a good deal more likely to be overlooked and forgiven in socially-effective people. In essence, the person with strong social skills and social self-confidence (non-shyness) is accorded many more chances to prove himself than is the shy, retiring person who commonly avoids informal social intercourse. Indeed, the latter type of person often makes work mates feel uncomfortable. And a technical error that would easily be overlooked or forgiven in the friendly, highly sociable employee is often viewed as cause for termination in the shy employee.

In order for a person to belong to informal social networks, he must be relaxed and easy to get to know. Dating is instrumental in promoting these interpersonal skills. Rare is the young man who is popular with women but unpopular among members of his own gender. The all-male peer group is extremely important in introducing its members to suitable female partners and in promoting informal dating and courtship.

Finally, ours is a coeducational world. To an increasing extent, women are successfully permeating all sectors of the work force. A male who has not learned to feel at home with women will encounter a never-ending array of anxiety-provoking situations in his career.

On Remedying Social Skills Deficits

Deficits in interpersonal skills are much more difficult to remedy in later life than are deficits in intellectual or in technical skills. A person can accumulate book-learning at any time of life. But the cultivation of expressive social skills cannot be effected through book learning nor can it be accomplished like intellectual learning at just any time of life.

Early Marriage and Professional Success

Columbia University sociologist Ely Ginzberg published a study in which he had followed for some fifteen years a large group of medical school graduates. During that time, all of the doctors had achieved professional success. But Ginzberg found that one of the strongest and least expected predictors of career success was the age at which a physician had married. Most Americans have long operated under the ascetic assumption that one of the sacrifices a person must make in order to become a medical doctor is to delay marriage. Not so, according to Ginzberg's findings.

Ginzberg divided the physicians into thirds in terms of how successful they were 15 years after graduation. The most successful third had married earliest in life, whereas the least successful had married latest. Indeed, several of the least successful had not married at all, whereas none of the most successful had remained unmarried. Moreover, a majority of the most successful had married while in their junior or senior undergraduate years, or in their first two years of medical school training.

Of course, early marriage is no guarantee of strong interpersonal skills. However, the evidence from the research of Jencks, Ginzberg and many others strongly suggests that early, successful heterosexual interaction does lead to the kind of social skills and social self-confidence that is as valuable in the world of employment as it is within the context of an individual's personal life.

Dating and General Happiness

The love-shy male of any age can usually think of little else than the mental-emotional prison blocking him from what he wants: female companionship. This fact was driven home to me several years ago in a study I conducted on the campus of the University of Utah in Salt Lake City. In this study dealing with the relationship between personality traits and all aspects of student behavior, a representative sample of more than 300 students was taken, and thousands of correlation figures obtained. A correlation coefficient is simply a barometer as to how strongly two factors are associated with each other. Of the thousands of correlation coefficients my study produced, the strongest was that relating these two variables: the degree of personal satisfaction with informal boy/girl interaction and general happiness.

Simply put, nothing in the entire study correlated more strongly with happiness and general sense of well-being than did extent of satisfaction with amount of informal boy/girl interaction. The correlation between these two factors was $+.65$ for the young men and $+.32$ for the young women.

A related correlation coefficient dealt with the relationship between general happiness and number of dates averaged per month. And this correlation figure was similarly far above average by social science standards—$+.49$ for males and $+.16$ for the females—another clear indication that women are far more important to men than men are to women.

Research has shown that happiness is a prerequisite for self-love, and that self-love is a prerequisite for a loving, caring attitude toward others. There is a kind of vicious circle here, because it is only through service to humanity that a person can achieve maximum happiness and contentment. As this book clearly demonstrates, love-shy males are often profoundly unhappy.

Why is the happiness of males more strongly influenced by

successful heterosexual interaction than that of females? Most researchers today believe that women can find emotionally intimate companionship vis-a-vis their own sex, whereas men can only satisfy their needs for emotional intimacy in the company of women. Furthermore, non-dating females normally manage to develop and maintain social skills and self-confidence in all-female peer groups, while non-dating males are usually isolated from social networks involving same-sexed peers.

Love as a Powerful Elixir

Further testimony to the destructive consequences of love-shyness comes from U.C.L.A.'s love laboratory. There appears to be a big difference, especially for men, between being involved in a mutually satisfying love relationship and an unrequited love or infatuation. Such romantic infatuation tends to be associated with such classic symptoms as loss of appetite, insomnia, inability to concentrate on work or studies, behavioral instability, a sharp dropping off in grades at school, inefficiency, uncooperativeness and aimlessness.

In contrast, the U.C.L.A. love researchers found mutual love relationships to be associated with a dramatically different kind of symptomology. Young men who were actively involved in mutual love relationships (wherein the girl interacted with and loved the young man in return), tended to be vibrant. This vibrancy and natural enthusiasm were associated with (1) better grades in school, (2) an increased capacity to concentrate, (3) better and more efficient use of time, (4) increased participation in social activities with their own gender, (5) better appetite, (6) an increased ability to sleep soundly, (7) an ability to remain effective with less sleep than they had required prior to falling in love, (8) improved overall health, (9) an increased attentiveness to all facets of personal appearance and grooming, and (10) an outward appearance and general ambiance that made their friends and acquaintances view them as looking better, more alive and vibrant, than they had formerly known them to be.

One of the most important findings to emerge from this

research was that (1) men who were involved in reciprocated love relationships tended to exude extremely bright, very strong Kirlian auras, whereas (2) men who were involved in unreciprocated infatuations tended to have very weak, "sick" auras.

Dr. Thelma Moss, one of America's most respected psi researchers, specializes in Kirlian photography. This is a form of electrical photography which permits the photographing of the human aura, the electromagnetic energy force field that suffuses the human body and holds it together. Dr. Moss had her laboratory in the same building as the love laboratory and she took advantage of the opportunity to photograph the Kirlian auras of (1) those in reciprocated love relationships, (2) those not in love, and (3) those involved in unrequited, unreciprocated infatuations.

Involvement in reciprocal love relationships was found to benefit women in much the same ways that it benefitted men. And this included the Kirlian aura. However, the findings were substantially weaker for the women than they were for the men. To be sure, the experience of being in love did not harm any of the women studied. But being in love tended to have a much more nearly neutral impact upon the women subjects than it had upon the male subjects.

In one significant respect the women studied were better off than the men. In particular, women were found to be substantially less susceptible than men to becoming involved in nonproductive, non-reciprocated romantic infatuations of the sort which the researchers found to give rise to the first quite negative set of symptoms.

Finally, when women did become involved in unreciprocated romantic infatuations, the effect upon their Kirlian auras tended to be minimal. In other words, unrequited love tended to very adversely affect the corona of a young man's Kirlian aura; the effect of unrequited love feelings upon a woman's aura tended to be minimal. On the other hand, active involvement in a *real* love relationship tended to galvanize a young man's Kirlian aura into a brilliant, full-bodied glow.

Active involvement in a genuine love relationship appears to constitute life-enhancing medicine for a young man. It represents rich fertilizer for the cultivation of social self-confidence and expressive interpersonal skills.

Normative Timetables of Self-Revelation

The "game" of dating and courtship holds no special allure for love-shy men. Most love-shy men prefer to bypass the "game" of dating and courtship and jump right into a permanent, binding relationship, foregoing the chase. Such outright candor early in a relationship frightens most women—particularly those used to the "game" of dating. They view the love-shy man as "weird" for expressing his desires too early in the relationship.

Further, love-shy men tend to renounce the masculine stereotype. They hate football, baseball, basketball, weight-lifting, beer-drinking, swearing and carousing with other men. They tend to be interested in the sorts of things women are interested in. Such openness is also frightening to women.

Premarital Virginity and Adjustment

Virginity in heterosexual males over the age of 20 is often a reflection of severe love-shyness and of interpersonal skill deficits. Sociologist Mirra Komarovsky found that 77 percent of the virginal men at Columbia University fell below the 50th percentile on national self-confidence norms as opposed to 34 percent for sexually-experienced men. Fully 78 percent of non-virginal men scored above the 50th percentile on leadership capacity, compared to 47 percent for the virgins. On sociability, 71 percent of the sexually-experienced men scored above the 50th percentile compared to 27 percent of the virginal men. And on self-acceptance, a mere 2 percent of non-virginal males scored below the 50th percentile on national norms as opposed to 47 percent of the virginal men.

To be sure, premarital sex (monogamous *or* promiscuous) does not cause a person to become self-confident, self-accepting, self-respecting, sociable, etc. In fact, 25 years ago most studies showed that sexually experienced women usually did not think as highly of themselves as did those who had managed to preserve their virginity. Today, on the other hand, most studies show that for single women as well as men beyond the age of 19, there is a positive relationship between monogamous premarital sexual experience and level of self-esteem. That positive relationship is usually found to be a good deal stronger for single males than for single females—because sexual experience is usually a good deal more important to the biological and emotional needs of single men than it is to single women. And the first sexual experience usually constitutes a major victory for most men. This is particularly true if it occurs within the context of a love relationship.

Parenthetically, young women (and even men) who are very casual in their premarital sexual activity usually have poorer levels of self-esteem than those whose premarital sex is kept monogamous and faithful. In other words, monogamous, loving, contraceptively-protected premarital sexual activity is usually found to be associated with high self-esteem. However, even promiscuous young men enjoy higher overall levels of self-esteem than socially inactive, virginal men.

I think the major reason for these findings is that virtually all heterosexually oriented young men want to have someone of the opposite sex to love. Those young men over the age of 20 who don't attain this goal are bound to develop increasingly poorer self-images and increasingly lower levels of self-esteem.

I fully realize that there are young men and women "out there" whose value systems prohibit premarital sexual activity. This comparatively small minority of young people will be able to sustain strong, healthy levels of self-esteem without premarital sex if and only if they manage to experience the joy of being involved in what for them is "the right man/woman relationship."

Chapter 2

The Biological Bases of Shyness

"If it is to be, it is up to me." This popular cliche represents the cornerstone of American ideology. The notion that severe shyness may be caused by inborn, biologically based factors, is anathema to many who want to believe they are in charge of their lives.

Given the nature of our American heritage, it is hardly surprising that not until the late 1960s did research studies get published on the inborn, biologically-rooted determinants of human personality. And even then, the work was spurred by rapid developments in Europe.

Thus, before 1970 parents were often blamed for childhood and adolescent autism, adult schizophrenia, and chronic depression. Shyness was seen as a neurotic condition, caused by faulty learning. Psychotherapy, behavior therapy, and behavior modification were marshalled to the rescue of shy people.

In the last decade, a great many studies have been published testifying to the biological basis of psychoses, such as schizophrenia, autism, and manic-depression and many neurotic conditions, including shyness.

But biological factors are not the only causes of shyness. It is the interaction between a person's biology and the forces which prevail in his cultural and social environment that make him what he is. In order to work, any therapy must take both into consideration.

Inborn Temperament

Obstetrical nurses, midwives and mothers have always known that people are not born alike. Some infants cry more than others. Some are noisy, others quiet. Some wriggle a lot while others stay motionless for long periods of time.

Such differences cannot be attributed solely to differences in quality of mothering, cleanliness, medical attention, feeding, or gender. Environmental and learning-related factors have been carefully controlled by many researchers. Yet these behavioral differences have been observed in healthy, well-loved and cared for infants long before any differential learning could take place.

Harvard University psychologist Jerome Kagan, in classic developmental studies, which commenced some 25 years ago, found that traits such as dependence, aggression, dominance and competitiveness did not remain consistent from age two or three to 20. But one trait did not change—behavioral inhibition. In unfamiliar situations afflicted children would display extreme caution; around strangers they would be demonstrably shy.

When they became adults, the inhibited subjects displayed unusually stable and high heart rates in response to mild mental stress. Kagan was intrigued by this finding; but steeped as he was in the prevailing behaviorist ideology of the day, he assumed he had simply detected an acquired fearfulness shaped by parents.

But when he and other researchers began finding apparent genetic differences in temperament from infancy onward between Chinese-American and Caucasian children, Kagan started in the mid-1970s to search for the biological underpinnings of the enduring trait of behavioral inhibition that he had stumbled on.

In 1979, Kagan and psychologists J. Steven Reznick and Nancy Snidman began following the development of extremely inhibited and demonstrably uninhibited children (using two groups, starting at 21 months of age in one group and 31 months of age in the other group). They tracked the children's heart rates and other physiological measures as well as observing their behavior in novel situations.

As of early 1988, they had studied these children through their seventh year. And although the shy children no longer behave exactly as they did at the age of two, they still display the pattern of very inhibited behavior combined with high physiological responsiveness to mild stress.

Along with their continuing and demonstrably high level of timidity, these children have been found to consistently manifest a pattern of physiological response to mildly stressful situations that do not faze their more advantaged, easygoing and relaxed peers. The responses include more dilated pupils, faster and more stable heartbeats, high salivary cortisol levels and brain/norepinephrine activity indicating that their sympathetic nervous system is revved up. These characteristics are so stable that Kagan, looking at the early indicators of behavioral inhibition at 21 months of age, can predict how children will score on several measures of stress reactivity at six years of age.

Kagan believes that very shy children tend to become uncertain and anxiety-ridden when placed in unfamiliar situations. It is now believed that this predisposition is related to the easily-aroused stress circuits of these inhibited children. As a case in point, inhibited toddlers quite commonly cling to their mothers and are very slow to venture into a strange though attractive playroom. According to Kagan these children case the environment very vigilantly; they tend to be highly self-conscious and to suffer from stage fright. Highly uninhibited (extroverted) children typically speak within the first minute upon entering a laboratory. In stark contrast, highly inhibited children will typically wait as long as 20 minutes before talking. Often conspicuously tense in posture and voice, the very shy children also perform worse than other children do on visual matching tasks, leaning either toward impulsivity (and wrong answers), or too much reflection and late answers.

At the Fels Institute located in Boston, a study was conducted by Dr. Kagan. There were seven boys who were noteworthy for being extremely inhibited and easily frightened during their first three years of life, the period during which they were intensively observed and studied. These children were all healthy and from good families. The key point is that they behaved in a consistently inhibited way. Dr. Kagan followed these boys until adulthood. And he found their temperaments in adulthood to be conspicuously different from those of other adult men in his study. All were heterosexual, but all were still very inhibited and "shy" in their informal interactions with others, particularly in the sort of ambiguous social situations where there is no role to play or script to follow.

As adults all seven of these men were particularly vulnerable to anxiety attacks and to various sorts of internal conflicts. None of them had pursued any sports or athletic activities, and none had pursued traditional masculine occupations, such as engineering or business. Two had become music teachers and one a psychologist.

Several studies in which Kagan had followed inhibited boys through adulthood clearly indicated that the ones who had been inhibited as three-year-olds tended to avoid dangerous or risk-taking activities, to show exceedingly little physical or verbal aggression, to display substantial timidity in social situations, to avoid sports, and to conform more than most children to their parents' wishes.

Mothers tend to report very timid children as having been demonstrably more colicky, constipated and easily irritated as infants than other children. Many have allergies that continued into middle childhood. In stark contrast, the uninhibited children in Kagan's study were found to be virtually allergy-free. Since shy people tend to have a surfeit of cortisol, and one of the major effects of this stress hormone is to suppress the body's immune system, Kagan believes that there is a close connection between high reactivity to stress and susceptibility to physical illness, especially head colds, and allergies.

Other evidence that humans inherit extreme shyness comes from behavioral genetics. Robert Plomin of Pennsylvania State University and David Rowe of the University of Oklahoma found that identical twins are likely to react in the same way to strangers. Working with psychologist Denise Daniels, Plomin used several personality and temperament questionnaires to compare 152 families who had adopted children with 120 families who were bringing up their own babies.

All of the parents rated their baby's shyness at 12 months and at 24 months. They described unfamiliar social situations the baby might encounter at home and reported on their own shy or outgoing temperament. Husbands and wives also rated each other. In addition, Plomin and Daniels asked the adopted babies' biological mothers to rate their own degree of shyness and sociability.

One of the most striking findings of this study, sponsored by the Colorado Adoption Project and published in 1955, was the strong resemblance between the degree of shyness of the biological mothers and that of the adopted babies at the age of 24 months (The babies had all been adopted within three months of birth).

This result is particularly impressive because the scores of the biological mothers are derived from questionnaires they had completed before the infants were born. Moreover, the infants' scores represented ratings by the adoptive parents more than two years later. Plomin and Daniels believe this is strong evidence of a genetic connection between the personalities of parents and their offspring.

In another investigation of twins, 79 pairs of monozygotic twins and 68 pairs of dizygotic twins, Irving Gottesman demonstrated a strong genetic component for social introversion or behavioral inhibition. Further, in a longitudinal twin study conducted by Robert Dworkin, the traits of anxiety-proneness and dependency were found to be highly heritable in teenagers and adults.

Probably the best-known research on the subject of identical twins reared apart is that which is being conducted at the University of Minnesota, under the direction of Thomas J. Bouchard, Jr. Bouchard's identical (monozygotic) twins had all grown up without any contact of any kind between each other. Throughout their respective childhoods most had not known that they had been adopted; yet many had intuitively "sensed" that they somehow had a twin somewhere.

Even though many of Bouchard's identical twins had never seen their twins for as many as 30 or more years after birth and had grown up virtually hundreds of miles apart, when they do first meet they often find that they married women/men of the same first name, physical description, career and education; they themselves have pursued the same education and career; they drive the same make and model of automobile; they own the same breed of dog and use the same name for their dogs; their children are of the same ages and genders and had been assigned the same first names; and their personality traits, behavioral dispositions and predilections are alike.

The range of similarities among these pairs of identical twins has been found to be absolutely astounding, and is in fact greater even than the range of similarities usually found for identical twins reared together in the same household. Identical twins reared together in the same home usually become highly motivated to "psychologically differentiate" and to manifest to the public a personal uniqueness. Twins reared apart without any knowledge of the fact that they have an identical twin are not thusly motivated. Nature is more easily permitted to take its course because each twin does not find it necessary to prove himself different from his identical twin. Therefore, identical twins reared apart are usually found to be more alike as adults than identical twins reared together in the same home.

Monkeys and Humans

While Kagan was conducting his early studies of child development during the 1950s and 1960s, the famed primatologist Harry Harlow was conducting his own now-classical research on infant rhesus monkeys' reactions to separation from their mothers. At the University of Wisconsin, Harlow showed that while some baby monkeys tended to become severely depressed on separation from their mothers, others emerged relatively unscathed from this experience. While working with Harlow during the late 1960s and 1970s, psychologist Stephen Suomi, now at the National Institute of Health, carefully focused his attentions on depression-prone monkeys—ones he later identified as "uptight." Suomi found that these monkeys displayed behavioral and physiological characteristics that resembled those of Kagan's timid and socially inhibited children.

During the first month of life, the uptight monkeys responded to the stress of a strange situation by being slow to explore. They also lagged behind in motor-reflex development and had poor muscle tone. During infancy, under the stress of brief separations from their mothers, these monkeys became less playful and showed the sharp rises in blood cortisol and the unusually high and stable heart rate that Kagan had observed in very shy human toddlers. These monkeys also displayed many signs of anxious behavior, such as clasping and grimacing, and had other physiological signs of stress.

Suomi had found that uptight monkeys, like Kagan's shy children, do not typically outgrow their abnormal physiological responses to stress. Those monkeys which, at the age of 22 days, had elevated blood cortisol levels in response to mild stress responded to such stress at the age of 18 months with the highest heart rates and blood cortisol levels in their age group. When these monkeys were later separated from their peers for periods of a week, they continued to show signs of anxious behavior and to have abnormal physiological responses. Once they were reunited, however, everything again appeared to be normal.

Even as late as adolescence—age four to five in rhesus monkeys—those monkeys which had been uptight during infancy continued to react abnormally to stress. But quite interestingly, as adolescents they tended to become hyperactive. As adults they tended to regress in the face of stress, showing the depressed behavior they had manifested during infancy.

Evidence that uptightness is probably inherited has been accumulating for several years now in Suomi's breeding colony. About one in four of these monkeys, descendants of Harry Harlow's monkeys, is born uptight. They are apt to be siblings or half-siblings rather than unrelated monkeys.

It is, of course, necessary to be cautious about the conclusions we derive from monkeys regarding humans. But we must not err on the side of being too cautious either. While not a perfect model of human behavior, rhesus monkeys share enough brain systems and social patterns with humans to make for some compelling comparisons. In addition, because monkeys develop faster than humans, four monkey generations can be compressed into the same time frame as one human generation, thus providing a long-range view of heredity and environmental interplay.

Because Stephen Suomi has carefully studied his monkeys over many generations, he knows their pedigrees, their childhood experiences, their adult behavior, and their individual characteristics. For example, he has found that monkey mothers, like humans, have varied styles of child-rearing. Some monkey mothers are quite nurturant and protect their offspring from stress, while others reject or ignore them. Some monkey mothers tend to be punitive, whereas others are indulgent, warm and loving. Such parenting styles tend to be fixed after the first baby is raised. Moreover, the mother's own temperament—whether relaxed or uptight—strongly affects the way she raises her babies. Independent of her genetic contribution to her infant's behavior, an uptight mother might pass on her own emotional tendencies to her offspring simply by providing a model of overreactive behavior or through her particular parenting style.

In order to test the relative influences of genetic endowment, caretaker style and caretaker temperament on infant behavior, Suomi subjects monkeys to foster parenting. He breeds uptight and relaxed monkeys, separates them at birth from their biological mothers and places them with substitute mothers chosen for various combinations of parenting styles and temperaments. For example, an uptight baby might be reared by a nurturant but uptight mother or by one who is relaxed but punitive.

In one such study, infant monkeys—half uptight and half relaxed—were assigned to foster mothers within one week of their births. Each caretaker-infant pair lived together except for a 20-minute separation once per week during the first month. While these infant monkeys were on their home turf with their foster mothers, the mothers' parenting style was the dominant influence on their behavior. Regardless of their inherited temperament, infants with punitive mothers tended to behave more anxiously than those reared by nurturant mothers.

But during the mildly-stressful separation periods, neither the mother's parenting style nor her temperament influenced the infant's behavior. Only inherited temperament predicted how the monkey would react to stress. Even with easygoing, nurturant mothers, uptight infants showed abnormal stress-reactivity.

After six months the baby monkeys were separated from their foster mothers for four-day periods, relieved by three-day reunions in the cage. Under these quite stressful conditions, heredity again asserted itself. For example, during separations the uptight monkey youngsters tended to become noticeably disturbed and passive in their behavior. And their blood-cortisol levels shot up far higher than those of their relaxed, easygoing peers. By the third or fourth separation, the temperamentally uptight monkey mothers also showed signs of anxiety.

At nine months the infants were separated from their caretakers and placed in peer groups where they are still being studied. While characteristically slow to adjust to these new circumstances, the uptight monkeys are for the most part thriving. In fact, according to Suomi's analysis, a few lucky enough to have been raised by nurturant mothers are now the dominant monkeys in their groups. This is a sure sign in monkey culture of social success!

But not surprisingly, the one unfortunate monkey who was triply handicapped—born with an uptight genetic structure and raised by a punitive and uptight foster mother—continues to struggle at the bottom of his peer group's dominance hierarchy.

A crucial question, of course, is how the naturally timid monkeys managed to overcome their handicaps and rise to the top of the social ladder. The answer, according to Suomi's analysis, is that these monkeys managed to cultivate the right social connections. In human terms, they managed to network properly.

More specifically, the uptight babies who eventually became dominant did so after Suomi introduced older females into the group to act as "foster grandparents." In natural groups out in the wild such older female monkeys are quite common. Thus, having learned to appreciate good parenting from their nurturant mothers, the uptight monkeys were quite possibly more motivated than their peers to seek out similar nurturant relationships with the older females. In the rhesus monkey matriarchy such relationships translate into power; and the lucky ones got it.

The "HPA Stress Circuit"

As has already been shown, when uptight monkeys and very shy human children have been subjected to stress, they have a tendency to show similar, abnormal physiological reactions. Most of these physiological reactions are also manifested by adults with symptoms of clinical anxiety and/or depression.

These atypical, physiological reactions center on a biological pathway that has come to be known as the "HPA axis" or as the "HPA stress circuit." In essence, this is the feedback loop which connects the hypothalamus in the lower brain with the pituitary and adrenal glands. Socially-stressful situations trigger in very shy people the following spate of important chemical events:

Chemical messengers such as the neurotransmitters serotonin, norepinephrine, and dopamine are sent to the hypothalamus, signaling it to secrete a corticotropin-releasing hormone. This in turn causes the pituitary gland, located just beneath the brain to release the adrenocorticotropin hormone (ACTH) into the bloodstream. The ACTH stimulates the adrenal glands to release the hormone cortisol into the bloodstream. Cortisol initiates a state of heightened bodily arousal that allows people to cope with the challenging situation. This aroused state is reflected in such measurable changes as increased heart rate, increased blood pressure, muscle tone and pupil dilation.

From early babyhood onward, as Jerome Kagan discovered, shys display an unusually intense response to mental and social stress, indicating that the sympathetic nervous system is keyed up. Their higher than normal salivary cortisol levels and brain-norepinephrine activity are typical of an over-reactive HPA stress circuit.

Very shy people, even under ordinary circumstances, have tended to show a well above average amount of the brain neuro-transmitter norepinephrine. Recent findings have also shown that the brains of very shy people do not metabolize sugar as well as or as efficiently as do the brains of non-shys.

Many clinicians are beginning to theorize that early deprivation of nurturant mother-love combined with stressful events may serve to render a genetically over-reactive HPA stress circuit even more hyper-reactive. Virtually all mothers verbally insist that they "love" their children. But researchers have learned that *feeling loved* is what really matters, *not* "being loved."

The physiological similarities between uptight monkeys and depressed humans have led researchers to examine how anti-depressant drugs might affect uptight infant monkeys. It was found that the drug imipramine (often employed to treat depression and anxiety attacks in humans) wields strongly calming therapeutic effects in anxious monkeys. In fact, young monkeys treated with imipramine and then separated from their peers (a major precipitator of stress in monkeys) play and explore significantly more than do their untreated uptight peers. Because it is stressful to them, separating monkeys from their peers acts to elevate norepinephrine activity in the brain. Imipramine acts to effectively lower this norepinephrine activity.

Three Neurotransmitters and Monoamine Oxidase

Of the more than 40 neurotransmitters, three are of special importance from the standpoint of differentiating extroverts from introverts: dopamine, norepinephrine, and serotonin. Highly inhibited, shy people tend to have too heavy a concentration in their brains of these, particularly of dopamine and norepinephrine. The greater the concentration of these three neurotransmitters, the more shy the person is likely to be. In contrast, the lower the concentration in the brain of these neurotransmitters (up to a certain point), the more extroverted the person is likely to be.

The monoamines, dopamine, norepinephrine, and serotonin, which serve as neurotransmitters or neuromodulators in the brain and central nervous system are involved in the control of basic neuropsychological processes, such as attention, memory, anxiety-proneness, and pain threshold.

Although brain amines cannot be studied directly in man, it is possible to infer their concentration by studying their metabolites in the cerebrospinal fluid, or the enzymes involved in their synthesis or degradation, such as monoamine oxidase (MAO).

Extroverts tend to have low levels of MAO in their brains, while shy, inhibited people tend to have very high levels. This finding constitutes a very important new development in our efforts to understand severe and chronic shyness. Moreover, it is no accident the MAO inhibitors have become the drug of choice in the treatment of anxiety/panic attacks—a condition that may well be biochemically and neurologically related to severe shyness.

Monoamines are one of the brain's natural "uppers". They constitute significant energy and morale boosters. In essence, too much monoamine *oxidase* serves to neutralize and destroy these "uppers", thus making a person depressed, behaviorally inhibited, low in energy, nervous and anxiety-prone. The key purpose behind the MAO inhibitor drugs is therefore to preserve enough of the brain's monoamines such that the person does not become unduly inhibited, anxious or depressed.

Brain Electrical Activity

Neuroscientist Dr. Eugene Redmond of Yale University, concluded from his research that panic, anxiety and fear may well be controlled by changes in norepinephrine metabolism in the locus coeruleus region of the brain. Locating an isolated brain area such as this (i.e., one that is vulnerable to the influences of substances in the blood due to its lack of a protective blood-brain barrier) provides us with potentially valuable information about the physiological roots of severe anxiety attacks, and of ultimately the fear of anxiety (anticipatory anxiety). In essence, it would appear from Redmond's studies that severe anxiety feelings may often result from a hyperactivity of the neurons in the locus coeruleus section of the brain.

Thus, Redmond implanted an electrode in the locus coeruleus section of the lower brain of a group of stumptailed monkeys. When this electrode was stimulated electrically, the monkeys behaved as if they were panicked, anxious, fearful, or in impending danger. In contrast, damaging this small brain center in the monkeys had the opposite effect. The monkeys without a functioning locus coeruleus showed an absence of emotional response to threats, and they were without apparent fear of approaching humans or dominant monkeys. Socially, they became much more aggressive; and they moved around in their cages much more than before, and more than normal monkeys.

In view of the fact that the locus coeruleus has the highest density of norepinephrine-containing neurons in the central nervous system, Redmond concluded from his work that panic and fear result from a hyperactivity of these neurons in the brain.

The fact that anxiety and fear could be switched on and off in this fashion conveys the idea of how physical the anxiety problem may well be. The site of the locus coeruleus is one of the most permeable areas of the brain, and hence it is one of the most sensitive areas to local metabolic changes. When the particular biochemical changes associated with severe anxiety feelings occur, this part of the brain may be the most sensitive to the changes and may be stimulated to produce its characteristic fear reactions.

Psychologist Hans J. Eysenck, long a major contributor to our knowledge of the biological bases of personality, concluded that inborn introversion is a natural byproduct of high native arousal levels in the cerebral cortex. These high arousal levels are caused by an overactive ascending reticular formation in the lower brain, which bombards the higher brain and central nervous system when stimuli perceived as socially threatening are presented. This inborn hyperarousability accounts for introverts' forming conditioned patterns of anxiety and other inappropriate emotional responses all too easily, and for their difficulty in extinguishing maladaptive conditioned responses.

Eysenck found that highly-extroverted people tend to have underaroused brains and nervous systems. They are stimulus hungry, always craving and seeking excitement.

Studies employing the electroencephalograph, or EEG which measures brain waves, have revealed large differences between introverts and extroverts that are apparent from early infancy and persist throughout life. The inhibited 10 percent of the population tend to have low amplitude and high frequency alpha waves typical of high arousal, whereas the extroverted 10 percent tend to have high amplitude and low frequency alpha waves, indicative of low arousal.

Thought and Brain Biochemistry

Up to this point I have stressed how native brain biochemistry and neurology may impact behavior and thought processes and create severe and chronic shyness/inhibition. However, there is another literature in psychology which suggests that the way we think can impact our brain biochemistry for good or for ill. Thought constitutes a powerful form of energy which can, under certain circumstances, operate to change and modify brain and body biochemistry. This is a central tenet of both self-image psychotherapy and of cognitive-emotive psychotherapy. This perspective is also highlighted in the frequently quoted Biblical passage: "According to your faith, so be it unto you."

Several of the recent works of popular author Norman Cousins (e.g., *Mind Over Illness*) show how morale can impact all aspects of human physiology and of physical and mental health. Cousins shows how he forced himself to think cheerful, happy thoughts, and how this effort thoroughly changed his medical prognosis for the better—quite to the surprise of many of the physicians who were attending him.

Playing a role can sometimes cause a person to become one with that role. This is true even when the role played is very different in nature from the personality to which a person is accustomed. For example, normally very vibrant, extroverted stage actresses have commented on how they have had to withdraw from a show after only a few months because the "downer" role they were playing was wrecking havoc upon their personal lives and social relationships. In the same way, putting on a happy face (facade) when one is "down" and upset can cause a person to begin to feel very happy and positive within only a short time of assuming that happy, upbeat role. Thus, actively pretending to be a socially self-confident person can over time and under certain circumstances actually lead to marked and very real increases in social self-confidence.

Of course, very shy people cannot bring themselves to pretend in this way as far as "real life" interaction is concerned—although many of them might be able to pretend within the artificial confines of a theatrical stage.

Right now very little is known about what specific conditions must be present in order for thought processes (e.g., positive versus negative mental attitude) to impact and change brain biochemistry/neurology. Monkeys have no way of deliberately directing the tenor and content of their thought processes. Many scientists believe that man *does* have a way of directing this.

Chapter Postscript

In a late 1988 issue of the journal *Developmental Psychology*, Avshalom Caspi, Glen H. Elder, Jr., and Daryl J. Bem published the results of a 30-year follow-up study of a large sample of shy and non-shy boys and girls. This quite remarkable study provides additional strong support for the point that shyness impacts the lives of boys/men far more severely than it impacts the lives of girls/women. This article ("Moving Away from the World: Life-Course Patterns of Shy Children") should be considered "must reading" for anyone interested in the subject of shyness. (See page 205 for complete reference.)

Chapter 3

Societal Reactions and Elastic Limits

Inborn temperament constitutes a kind of limit, just as native intelligence represents a kind of limit within which a person must function throughout his or her life. The little boy who has high inborn inhibition and a low anxiety threshold, if subjected to the conventional all-boy peer group, will be unlikely to develop the interpersonal skills necessary for happy survival. On the other hand, if that boy is introduced to a group of both boys and girls who are temperamentally similar and is not subjected to frightening games or to bullying, he is likely to grow up well adjusted. In fact, child development psychiatrists Alexander Thomas and Stella Chess have shown that such a boy's chances for success will be about as good as those of children born with more outgoing temperaments.

The "Wish Bone Effect"

Visualize a class of 100 kindergarten boys, all aged five, all starting on the same day. Some of these children will come from warmer, more loving homes than others will. Some will feel more loved than others. Every class of children has its stars, children who

FIGURE ONE
The Wish Bone Effect

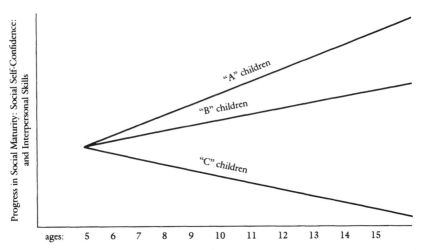

exude self-esteem. The letter "A" in figure one represents these 15 lucky little boys.

Just as every class contains its stars, it also contains a certain number of children who exude a so-called negative social stimulus value caused by behavioral inhibition, physical unattractiveness, and parents who don't make them feel loved. We will assume that these children have normal intelligence and health. The letter "C" represents these five children in the diagram.

The remaining 80 children that fall in between the two extremes are represented in our diagram by the letter "B." Throughout the formative years of elementary school each boy of this majority group makes good, steady progress in the growth and development of interpersonal skills, social self-confidence, and social maturity.

The numbers running along the bottom of Figure One represent chronological ages ranging from five to 15. All three lines begin at age 5 and reflect progress in social/emotional growth, and in level and adequacy of interpersonal skills.

The major point of the hypothetical diagram is that the rich get richer while the poor get poorer. This cliché is as valid in understanding the development of social self-confidence, interpersonal skills and social/emotional maturity as it is in understanding the development of financial fortunes. The three lines all start out at the same point. Yet with each passing year, the distance between them grows greater and greater.

The B people, who are progressing normally, move steadily upward from one chronological age to the next. The ever increasing distance between lines A and B, and B and C, indicates that the social stimulus value of both the A children and the C children is growing stronger each passing year.

The star quality of the As continues to improve relative to their classmates. The C children become increasingly conspicuous with each passing year. Indeed, the distance between the C and the B children is substantially greater than that between the Bs and the As.

The C boys withdraw from their fellows' invitations to play. They prefer more quiet play at the craft tables with the girls. They refuse to defend themselves when punched or bullied, seeking the teacher's protection. The more frequently the C boys follow this avoidant course of action, the more conspicuous they become vis-a-vis their classmates. They develop reputations as fair game to bully because they won't fight back. The more they suffer, the more they are bullied.

Psychologist Howard Kaplan, who has done a good deal of experimental research on aggression, concludes that aggression is more likely to occur if the victim is perceived as unwilling or unable to retaliate. And this is exactly the position of the C children. Physically aggressive retaliation is not in keeping with their native temperaments. They cannot understand the feelings and the motives of the B children; and the B children cannot understand them.

Meanwhile these C children are gradually learning to run home right after school and to avoid all informal social activity. Being near peers when a supervising adult is not around to protect them is potentially painful and dangerous. They are discouraged from playing wth girls, and they cannot play with boys. There are no "gentle" sports and games available to them. So they become isolates.

As the C boys grow older their deficits in interpersonal skills become ever greater, thus making them more and more adversely conspicuous. And the more conspicuous they become, the more often they are bullied—or ignored.

Since all human beings require some sort of attention and recognition, some of the C boys may become class clowns. As negative attention is usually less painful than no attention at all, some of the Cs develop unhealthy defense mechanisms, further alienating them from the group. And the more alienated they become, the more emotionally immature they appear to others. By the time they are teenagers, their level of interpersonal skills and social-emotional maturity will be extremely poor compared to the adjusted children in their class. By that time, many of them will be labeled weird or even gay.

For the A boys the same mechanism operates except in the reverse way. At the outset they are more attractive, friendly, and capable than most of the other boys, so everyone wants to play with them. And since everyone wants to be with them, they gradually develop a strongly positive, robust self-image and social self-confidence. Their interpersonal skills grow as the years pass; they mature socially. By the time they enter adolescence, they are likely to be class officers. They are pursued by girls.

The inborn social stimulus value created by native temperament and physical attractiveness serves to get young boys started on either the right foot or on the wrong foot relative to their peers. As Figure One illustrates, those who commence school at age five with an adverse social stimulus value tend to be avoided, ignored, or bullied. Consequently, they learn to avoid people; and they learn to associate the very thought of informal socializing with thoughts of mental pain and anguish. As such, their interpersonal-skill deficits and their social self-confidence deficits relative to their peers become worse and worse.

This is how boys become chronically love-shy adults. Yes, the shyness itself is learned, but inborn temperament provides the indispensable prerequisites and catalysts for negative learning to get under way in the first place.

The Sociological Perspective

The "looking-glass self" theory of sociology is applicable here. A child sees a kind of reflection of himself in his social looking-glass and internalizes the messages that he receives from this social mirror. When his social mirror consistently feeds back ego-disparaging, caustic and unkind messages, the sense of self rapidly becomes one with those messages. The child's self-esteem suffers irreversible damage.

Intellectually, the child may fully think that he believes the old adage "sticks and stones may break my bones but names will never hurt me." But research has shown that the conative or emotional (subconscious) part of man's brain influences him more strongly than the cognitive or intellectual (conscious) part. So the name-calling has a cumulative impact, causing the child to develop poor self-esteem.

Every Group Needs a Deviant

For many years now sociologists have argued that every group of five or more persons needs a deviant, or nonconformist. Seeing the deviant get punished or ostracized for his behavior tends to enhance the awareness of all group members of the prevailing norms. That tends to make each group member become more uncritical and accepting of those norms.

This is certainly true for norms regarding masculine behavior. For example, some 30 years ago, social psychologist Muzafer Sherif conducted what has become a classic study—group behavior in 10-year-old boys at a summer camp in Connecticut. For the study he recruited about 100 boys, all of whom were the leaders in their fifth-grade classrooms. Each boy was given a free five-week stay in a summer camp. All were normal boys, highly sociable and uninhibited.

Shortly after their arrival at the camp, the boys, who were strangers on arrival, were divided up into groups of 12 boys each. Within three days, each group had begun to develop a pecking order. For the first time in their lives, some of the boys were bullied, teased, and ostracized. One group singled out a boy for the deviant role because of the shape of his head—and they called him "lemon head." Another group singled out a boy because he was not considered fast enough—even though back home that boy had been faster than any of his classmates.

Even when all the members of a group are considered normal in one setting, some will be singled out in a new setting as a new pecking order is formed. Many of the boys who had been popular and respected back in their fifth-grade classrooms, now found themselves at the middle or low end of the group. Not everyone can be at the top.

If a deviant can be recruited within three days by a group of well-adjusted and well-respected leaders, it is easier to understand how easy it is for school boys to recruit a behaviorally-inhibited, isolated classmate for the deviant role.

Chapter 4

How the Information Was Obtained

The purpose of this chapter is two-fold: (1) to provide a clear and succinct summary of the major personal characteristics of the love-shy and of the non-shy samples, and (2) to provide a brief, easily understandable statement as to how the research data were obtained. In a book of this nature it would be inappropriate to provide an elaborate discussion of statistical and methodological issues and procedures. Nevertheless, the reader should have an accurate awareness of the nature of the people studied. Such an awareness will render my discussion of the research results far more interesting and meaningful than could otherwise be the case.

Who Are the Love-Shy?

All love-shy men are virgins; they rarely or never go out socially with women; they have never had an emotionally close, meaningful relationship with a woman; they suffer emotionally because of this lack. They desperately want to have a viable relationship but are too shy; they become extremely anxiety-ridden over the mere thought of asserting themselves vis-a-vis a woman in a casual, friendly way; and they are strictly heterosexual.

Distinguishing Heterosexuals from Homosexuals

In order for my research to make any sense, I had to be certain that my samples of love-shy men did not include any homosexuals. This is an important issue because young men who are heterosexually inactive and who do not participate in conventional courtship activities are often viewed as "homosexually inclined."

Most social scientists agree that the following four criteria distinguish heterosexuals from homosexuals.

1. A heterosexual's romantic fantasies and daydreams are directed towards people of the opposite sex.
2. Heterosexuals always fantasize about being with a female partner when they masturbate.
3. Heterosexuals strongly prefer having sexual intercourse with a woman to the idea of experiencing sex with a man.
4. Heterosexuals must define themselves as heterosexuals.

Early in each interview questions were asked pertaining to the foregoing points. If a respondent displayed any ambivalence with respect to any of the four issues, the interview was terminated. Thus, respondents whose heterosexuality was in doubt were simply not used.

Interestingly, 94 percent of the love-shy men were strong believers in homosexual rights. Yet, every single one indicated disgust at the mere thought of kissing or making love to another man.

Romantic interests and fantasies crop up earlier than sexual ones—sometimes during elementary school years. Moreover, these romantic interests are strongly influenced by esthetic considerations (i.e., a pretty face). Studies of the childhoods of hundreds of homosexuals have revealed that most became infatuated with the pretty faces of certain boys around the ages of 10 or 11. At such early ages, sexual fantasies tend to be absent. At such early ages most pre-homosexuals had no idea they were displaying interest patterns placing them in a homosexual social category.

Heterosexual love-shy males appear to develop a sense of beauty significantly earlier in life than do most other people of either gender. This predilection for beauty seems to be a driving need for many of them. Several of the love-shys told me that even when they were third-grade youngsters they could remember not being able to concentrate in class because of fantasies about little girls. In addition to the love-shys' distaste for the rougher play of the all-male peer group, they avoided the group because it did not contain any pretty people.

One of the strongest indicators of male homosexuality is that of being more interested in sex play with boys than with girls: 78 percent of adult homosexuals in one study said that they had felt this way as children, whereas 82 percent of adult heterosexuals said that they had not felt this way as children. In the study on which this book is based, not one love-shy man out of the 300 surveyed had ever had any preference at all during childhood for sex play with boys over sex play with girls. Furthermore, not a single one of the 300 love-shys had ever had any actual sex play experience during childhood or adolescence with a member of either gender. As children, many of the men I interviewed had wanted to enjoy sex play with a girl, but not surprisingly simply did not have the nerve to try.

In short, social withdrawal appears to be the key earmark of the love-shy. Even though the love-shy are clearly heterosexual in their preferences and orientations, they engage in significantly less heterosexual sex play during childhood and adolescence than do the non-shy. Interestingly, fully 23 percent of the 200 non-shy heterosexuals interviewed for this book had engaged in some homosexual sex play with their male peers as young teenagers. In contrast, not a single one of the 300 heterosexual love-shy men had ever done this. And not a single one had ever wanted to. Indeed, all indicated that in childhood as in adulthood they had been revolted at the thought.

Finally, most homosexual males become aware of their romantic-sexual attraction to other males sometime between their tenth and thirteenth years. It has been found that almost all become aware of this attraction by the time their seventeenth birthday rolls around. The 300 love-shy men and the 200 socially self-confident men studied for this book were all well beyond their seventeenth year in chronological age. Hence, there can be little doubt as to the true heterosexuality of all of the 500 men who were investigated.

Three Samples Were Studied

Three samples of men were obtained for this research. These were as follows:

1. 100 single, never married love-shy men, all of whom were between the ages of 35 and 50 at the time they were interviewed.

2. 200 single, never married love-shy men, all of whom were fulltime university students between the ages of 19 and 24 at the time they were interviewed.

3. 200 single, never married men who were self-confident and non-shy with the opposite sex. These 200 men were all fulltime university students between the ages of 19 and 24.

This non-shy comparison group was composed of people who were similar to the love-shys in social and demographic character-istics. All of them viewed themselves as above average in social self-confidence vis-a-vis members of the opposite sex. The presence of a comparison group helps researchers make educated and reasoned deductions about the major causes behind a phenomenon. The more we know about causes, the better able we are to predict, control, cure and possibly even prevent the phenomenon from occurring in the future.

Ideally it would have been desirable to have included a second comparison group in the 35- to 50-year-old bracket. I chose not to include such a comparison group because the majority of non-shy heterosexual men in that age bracket are married and no longer involved with the various problems of dating and courtship. In fact, their interaction with women is significantly limited by marriage. A sample of widowed and separated men would not have been repre-sentative of well-adjusted, non-shy men in the 35 to 50-year-old age range.

Limiting the comparison group to single, never married young men in the 19- to 24-year-old age range served this study well in providing the required contrast. By comparing and contasting the backgrounds of the non-shys with those of the love-shys, it became feasible to arrive at meaningful conclusions as to what the key causes of love-shyness probably are. In virtually every comparison that was made, the younger love-shys differed from the non-shys in the same way as the older love-shys differed from the non-shys. The differences which are highlighted between the non-shys and the love-shys are real differences, which are likely to have a strong bearing on the causes of love-shyness.

How the Respondents Were Obtained

Younger Love-Shy Group

The 200 19- to 24-year-old men came from seven university campuses in the greater New York and Los Angeles metropolitan areas, with the exception of 25 respondents who were interviewed at a university in the Deep South.

Bulletin board announcements placed in classroom buildings, dormitories and off-campus laundromats briefly described the nature of the study and the type of respondents (including the six criteria of love-shyness) that were sought. The announcements included mention of a $10 payment for individuals serving as research respondents.

I was already aware that love-shy people seldom have telephones, finding it too threatening even to make business calls. So the bulletin-board announcements requested interested men to write to me.

Because I was inviting responses from severely shy young men who often harbor strong inhibitions against self-disclosure, I wanted to make the announcements as non-threatening and inviting as possible. I also wanted to arouse the love-shys' curiosity. I therefore pointed out that I was a licensed therapeutic counselor in the state of California and that I was particularly interested in finding ways to restructure the social system so as to better meet the needs of love-shy men. Hence, the announcements stated that love-shys had long been ignored by politicians, university and college administrators and social event coordinators; and that the time had finally come to do something constructive to remedy this situation.

The bulletin board method worked, although progress was slow. As letters trickled in, each respondent was contacted in person and screened. Some were not included in the study because they did not fit any of the six delineated love-shyness criteria. But, more than 80 percent did fit the criteria and were eventually interviewed, in most cases within a few days of their responses.

Though three hours were set aside to interview candidates, many interviews ran beyond four hours. People with strong inhibitions about self-disclosure often open up when they are with someone who shows a sincere interest in them and who lets it be known that he is looking for ways to catalyze society into helping love-shy people.

I personally conducted all the interviews for the study. With some respondents, two, three or even four letters preceded the interview. Some needed assurances. And in some cases appointments had to be changed or confirmed.

The Older Love-Shy Group

The older love-shy group was composed of 100 virginal, single, never married men in the 35- to 50-year-old category. My original intention had been to find 200 older love-shys. But inquiries came in so slowly, I decided that it would be better to cut the sample off at 100 men than to wait two or three years to find the rest.

Like the younger love-shys, each of the 100 older men had all six love-shy characteristics. But because they were older, they had lived with their conditions much longer. Whereas some of the younger love-shys were still optimistic about their life chances, most of the older ones seemed quite pessimistic about their love-shyness and cynical about the world in general and particularly about women.

Most of the men, 78, came via the bulletin-board announcements, while 22 came via the owner of a New York area commercial dating service. Announcements were placed on the bulletin boards of a large number of laundromats throughout the greater Los Angeles and New York metropolitan areas. Announcements indicated that respondents were needed for a study on severe shyness in informal man/woman situations. The announcements stated that the study was concerned with men in the 35- to 50-year-age range who were still single, not out of choice but because of chronic and severe shyness. As with the younger love-shys, the announcements made clear the point that only heterosexual men were wanted.

The Socially Self-Confident, Non-Shy Men

The announcements to attract non-shy men did not indicate that respondents were to comprise a comparison group or that the research subject was love-shyness. I felt that mentioning shyness might serve to turn off potentially good respondents. The research was described as involving young men who engage in a great deal of heterosexual interaction, including dating, partying, love-making, etc. The $10 reward was also mentioned. Potential respondents were asked to get in touch with me by phone.

Inquiries from non-shys came at a much faster pace than they came in from the love-shys. This was to be expected, given the anxieties of the love-shy males. The result was that I could have chosen all 200 non-shy men from the same university. However, I decided that the best comparison group would be composed of young men from the same seven universities as the love-shys. I also decided that each university should contribute approximately the same number of respondents to each category. This was successfully accomplished.

Only 6 of the 200 non-shys (three percent) were virginal. Thus, 97 percent of the socially self-confident non-shys were sexually experienced. A majority had had a considerable amount of premarital coital experience. Most of the non-shys experienced premarital sex in a number of stable, monogamous relationships. Most had been involved in three or four relationships, with 53 percent cohabiting with a girl for six months or more and 38 percent cohabiting at the time they were interviewed.

Chapter 5

Intrauterine Antecedents

On the surface, Communist East Germany would seem to be one of the least-likely places to produce important research findings pertinent to love-shyness. However, for many years East German officials have been endeavoring to gain distinction for their country by getting their youths to score highly in the Olympic Games.

Towards this end East Germany does everything in its power to involve youth, especially young boys, in demanding athletic activity as early in life as possible. The goal of the East Germans is to produce outstanding athletes. And boys who for whatever reason perform inadequately at physical activity, and/or who display less than an enthusiastic attitude, interest, and motivation with respect to such activity, remain at the bottom of the social status and prestige-ladder among their peers and vis-a-vis the adult community as well.

Because such masculine activities are important to the East Germans, they have tried to find out why some boys remain uninterested in athletics, and whether anything can be done to get them interested. With respect to the second question the East Germans learned early in their investigations that the application of psychological pressure often made matters worse rather than better.

47

The children tended to become even more disinterested in spite of burgeoning social unpopularity and ever increasing public ostracism from peers and coaches. To try to understand this "unnatural" attitude, the East Germans probed the anatomy, physiology, and body biochemistry of the nonconformists. Rather than turning to psychology for answers, as Americans do, the East Germans looked first to the medical laboratory for answers.

Blood Testosterone

The first finding the East Germans uncovered was that many nonconforming boys had below-average amounts of the male hormone testosterone in their blood. This was especially true for boys of normal size and weight.

At first they thought they had uncovered a biochemical basis for homosexuality; but, it turned out that very few of the low-testosterone boys grew up to become homosexuals. In fact, homosexuality turned out to be just slightly more common among low-testosterone boys than among those with normal levels. As young adults, the low-testosterone males took longer than their peers in finding female partners.

The most remarkable finding was the strong relationship between a pregnant woman's personality and her male fetus' blood testosterone level. Personality traits, such as tenseness, irritability, depression, nervousness, and volatility had the effect of neutralizing testosterones and/or related enzymes in the developing fetus and thus of feminizing it.

Girl fetuses carried by the same kind of mothers developed normally, since the absence of male hormones has no effect on them.

The notion that the mind affects the body is not new. Psychosomatic and holistic medicine have been expanding enormously in recent years. But what has been ignored until now is that what goes on in the mind of a pregnant woman affects the fetus. If a pregnant woman is tense, nervous, irascible or depressed, she is likely to give birth to a feminized (pre-shy) boy baby.

The East Germans also found that a relaxed, fun-loving,

happy-go-lucky woman will typically give birth to a highly-masculine baby.

These traits in a mother's personality are also bound to affect her child after birth. Irritable and tense mothers may even provoke love-shyness by rendering boys fearful and distrustful of getting close to a woman. Negative maternal personality traits have a strong impact on the inborn biology and physiology of a boy child. And this is true quite irrespective of genetic considerations.

Enzyme Activity and Propitious Fetal Growth

Research currently being conducted in human biochemistry and physiology suggests that a malfunctioning enzyme may be a major cause of severe love-shyness. Enzymes are functionally indispensable to the normal growth and development of all living organisms.

For example, prepubescent boys and girls have about the same ratio of estrogens to testosterones in their bloodstreams. The pituitary gland and perhaps the pineal gland serve to govern the time clock that determines when the appropriate enzymes will be released to stimulate secondary sex characteristics. Enzymes enable hormones to promote these growth changes.

Many biochemists and physiologists now believe that a number of enzymes crucial to the development of masculine assertiveness, competitiveness and drive are released sometime during the second trimester of pregnancy in a male. These enzymes permit the testosterones to work on various sections of the brain that nature has programmed to be responsive to these male hormones. If an enzyme malfunctions, the part of the brain affected by that enzyme will not be suitably masculinized.

Some sections of the brain control sexual/romantic directionality. When these brain sections are inadequately masculinized, the person stands a good chance of becoming a homosexual or bisexual. When brain areas concerning effeminacy are not masculinized, the person may become effeminate. Contrary to popular impression, most effeminate men are not homosexual; most will marry and become fathers. But because of gender role expectations for males, they will suffer teasing and hazing throughout their formative years as a result of the effeminacy.

Another section of the brain directing social assertiveness and competitive drive has a strong bearing on shyness generally and on love-shyness in particular. The nonassertive, unaggressive little boy will commonly develop non-masculine interest patterns. He violates traditional gender role expectations in terms of interests. For example, he prefers quiet, non-physical forms of play, arts and crafts, music and theatre arts, dolls and figurines, etc., all of which violate gender role expectations.

To be sure, occasionally a number of different fetal enzymes will malfunction, causing a male child to develop a number of different problems. For example, he may develop both effeminacy and homosexuality, or both effeminacy and chronic shyness or chronic shyness and homosexuality. In a few rare cases, he may develop all three problems.

The Neurotransmitters and Testosterone

East German biochemist Gunter Dorner recently published research showing that testosterone has a profound effect on the brain's three major neurotransmitters: serotonin, dopamine, and norepinephrine, the neurotransmitters discussed in Chapter Two, which exert a strong impact on behavioral inhibition, mood and proneness to anxiety.

The sex hormones, and particularly testosterone, greatly influence brain development, brain structure, and ultimate behavior. Bruce McEwen, a neurobiologist at the Rockefeller University in New York City, has discovered that the fetus has brain receptors for each sex hormone during a critical period of development in precisely those areas of the brain which are now believed to organize differences in gender behavior, such as the female tendency to avoid stress and the male tendency to be assertive, competitive and aggressive.

Recent research strongly suggests that it is the operation of the sex hormones *in utero* that is of enormous importance in a person's ultimate social behavior and preferences.

Prenatal Hormones and Fetal Feminization

Anke A. Ehrhardt and Heino Meyer-Bahlburg at Columbia University have shown the importance of the hormonal environment of the uterus. They looked at children whose mothers had been given hormones to maintain pregnancy. Girls exposed intrautero to testosterone-based progestogens tended to become more tomboyish and energetic than the large majority of unaffected girls. The affected boys were also found to be much more energetic and aggressive than their peers.

In contrast, progesterone-based progestogens had a demonstrably demasculinizing impact whether administered alone or in combination with estrogens. Boys exposed to them as fetuses were found as children to be conspicuously less aggressive and assertive, to display poorer athletic coordination and lowered masculine interests than their peers. Girls whose mothers had been treated with progesterone-based progestogens were less active, less verbally aggressive, and less given to energetic play than their peers. Further, both boys and girls preferred female friends.

All of the evidence to date clearly indicates that in humans as well as in monkeys, sex hormones operating in the uterus on the developing brain are responsible for what might be called a pretuning of the personality. The sex hormones organize the social demeanor of the sexes, their orientation to the problems of life and the way they go about solving them.

Whereas some receptors govern sexual orientation, others relate to sex-appropriate behaviors and interests. Evidently, in some male fetuses, the latter can be adversely affected without damaging sexual-preference receptors. We are still a long way from understanding how all of these processes work. However, numerous interesting hints have been issuing from the work of Gunter Dorner. Dorner observed that rats could be rendered homosexual if deprived in the womb of testosterone during the critical period of brain differentiation. When these rats became adults, Dorner injected them with estrogen. His argument was that if the brains of these rats had been feminized in the intrauterine environment, then their brains would respond as if to a signal from a nonexistent ovary with a surge of ovulation-inducing hormone—the so-called luteinizing hormone (LH). And they did so. Their brains had indeed been feminized.

Dorner then applied this technique to human male homosexuals, and he found the same thing. Their brains responded with a hormonal surge whereas the brains of a sample of heterosexual males did not.

During this time Ingeborg Ward at Villanova University, had been showing that if you subjected pregnant female rats to stress, their male offspring would have extremely low levels of testosterone at birth and would exhibit feminized and demasculinized sexual behavior in adulthood. In essence, they would become bisexual or homosexual and would display passive, shy, socially-withdrawn behavior. Dorner repeated her experiment and then looked at the human population to see if there might be a connection between parental stress and male homosexuality.

First Ward looked at the records to see whether more male homosexuals had been born during the stressful period of World War II than had been born either before or after it. And she found a very high peak during 1944 and 1945. Dorner then interviewed a sample of 100 homosexual and bisexual men matched with a sample of 100 heterosexual men. And she found that more than two-thirds of the mothers of the homosexuals and bisexuals had been under moderate to quite severe stress during the period when they had been pregnant. In contrast, only about 10 percent of the mothers of the heterosexual men had been under stress, and most of their stress had been mild by comparison.

On the basis of these and other data, Dorner concluded that male homosexuality is a result of permanent neurochemical changes in the hypothalamus that are effected by reduced levels of testosterone during fetal life. This produces a feminization of the brain which is activated, as far as sexual behavior/interests are concerned, at puberty. The data indicate that stress in the mother is a major risk factor causing the production of substances in the adrenal glands which act to depress testosterone levels in the male fetus. This and other related factors operate to permanently alter the neural circuitry of the brain, the nerve pathways that are controlled by the local brain hormones, the neurotransmitters (serotonin, dopamine, and norepinephrine). Further, these three neurotransmitters appear to be the local mediators of the effects the sex hormones (particularly testosterone) have on brain cells, and on behavior, throughout life.

As we have seen, one clear way in which heterosexual love-shyness differs from male homosexuality is that the activated sexual interests in love-shys at puberty are exclusively heterosexual in nature. However, both before and after puberty male love-shys strongly prefer the idea of playing with girls as opposed to playing with boys. And their recreational interests tend to be demonstrably feminine as far as our cultural definitions are concerned.

Further, heterosexual love-shys appear to have always been deeply romantically oriented both before as well as after pubescence. This strong, preadolescent need for pair-bonding with a romantic lover does not appear to be a consistent earmark of homosexual males. This is why it is prudent to speculate upon the existence of different sex hormone receptors in the brain which respond to these chemicals during intrauterine life.

Maternal Stress and the Neurotransmitters

It is now possible to demonstrate that the levels of serotonin, dopamine and norepinephrine are quite dramatically altered in different areas of the brain as a result of prenatal stress in both male and female rats. In fact, it has recently been shown that as adults the female offspring of prenatally-stressed mothers have altered levels of these neurotransmitters and poor reproductive capacity, manifested by irregular estrus cycles, low sexual receptivity, difficulty becoming pregnant, tendency to spontaneously abort and failure to produce sufficient milk for offspring. To be sure, extrapolating from rats to man is always risky. But these research results must be viewed as strongly suggestive.

Critical Periods

Bob Goy of the primate research lab at the University of Wisconsin, has highlighted four ways in which male rhesus monkeys at young ages differ in their behavior from females: they are more prone to initiate play, roughhouse, mount peers of both sexes and mount their mothers.

But, Goy has been able to cause the same behavior in young females by giving their pregnant mothers injections of testosterone. As a result of such treatment, the young females play rough and act assertively.

Many of Goy's testostereone-treated female monkeys tend to be born with somewhat masculinized genitals. Thus, there is clearly a critical prenatal period for the formation of genitals. But far more interesting is the fact that there also appears to be a critical period for each of the four sex-specific behaviors delineated above.

My Own Findings

As a social scientist I could not test the blood testosterone levels of the 500 men studied. Nor could I get blood samples from the men in utero. Still my study turned up a substantial amount of data that lend support to the proposition that severely love-shy males had been feminized while in the womb. Most of my love-shy respondents had been born to mothers characterized by tenseness, irascibility, cantankerousness, high irritability and depression. Moreover, an unusually high proportion of these mothers had had significant problems during their pregnancies.

For example, I asked each respondent whether or not his mother had had any miscarriages either before or after he was born. Only 12 percent of the non-shy men responded in the affirmative compared to 26 percent of the younger love-shy men and 31 percent of the older ones. When asked whether or not the mother had ever had any stillbirths, 42 percent of the older love-shys and 36 percent of the younger ones responded in the affirmative, compared to only five percent of the non-shy men.

Miscarriages and stillbirths are important to our understanding of the etiology of love-shyness because they may represent a psychosomatic reflection of the woman not wanting a child. Secondly, hormones taken by increasing numbers of pregnant women have been found to cause mild degrees of hermaphroditism in growing fetuses.

The second point may be one of considerable importance. For many years now, female hormones have been prescribed as a means of preventing miscarriages and stillbirths. I had no way of finding out whether or not the love-shys' mothers had taken female hormones during the course of their respective pregnancies. But since 31 percent of the mothers of the older love-shys were prone to miscarriage compared to only 12 percent of the non-shys' mothers, there is at least some possibility that a few of the love-shy men might have been feminized by female hormones.

I also asked each man if his mother had a baby that died within a few days or a week of its birth. Fully 47 percent of the older and 44 percent of the younger love-shys indicated that it had happened once or more. None of the non-shys gave me a similar response.

Birth is a painful experience for most if not all women. Yet the large majority of women seldom if ever complain about it. Even fewer women complain to their children about such pain. Nature seems to have a way of making most women forget the pain and discomfort accompanying childbirth.

Nevertheless, I asked each respondent whether his mother had complained a lot about the pain and stress she had suffered and endured while giving birth to him. While none of the non-shy men responded in the affirmative, 16 percent of the older love-shys and 12 percent of the university-aged love-shys replied in the affirmative.

Better than 25 percent of the love-shy men took longer to be born than most babies compared to only four percent of the non-shy men.

None of the non-shy men had been born prematurely, while 15 percent of the love-shy men had. None of the non-shy men had been delivered by Caesarean section, whereas 12 percent of the love-shy men had been. Twenty-nine percent of the older love-shys and 23 percent of the younger ones recalled that their mothers had had an unusually long and painful menopause in contrast to only four percent of the non-shys.

Love-Shys as Quiet Babies

Each man was asked to react to the statement: "My mother used to comment from time to time that I was a rather quiet baby, and that I didn't cry very much." If the love-shys agreed with this statement to a significantly greater extent than the non-shys, it would provide further support for one or both of these positions: that the intrauterine stage had had a feminizing effect on them and that they had been born with the behavioral inhibition gene with its accompanying hyperactive "HPA stress circuit" and surfeit of dopamine, serotonin, norepinephrine and monoamine oxidase.

Only 16 percent of the non-shy men agreed that their mothers had commented that they had been quiet babies, compared to 86 percent of the older love-shys and 73 percent of the younger. Because the love-shys often did not get on well with their mothers, it seems unlikely that the mothers would cast praise on their children for having been quiet babies—unless they indeed really had been unusually quiet.

Mothers' Personalities

I asked numerous questions about the mothers' personalities. For example, 35 percent of the love-shys said their mothers were extremely tense, high strung, and apt to burst into rages—the same personality traits that the East Germans related to feminized boys. In contrast, only four percent of the non-shys remembered their mothers as having been this way.

Another representative question is the following: "My mother was always easily angered and very prone to outbursts of temper." Better than 50 percent of the love-shys responded in the affirmative, compared to just 20 percent of the non-shy men. And to the statement: "My mother was always a patient person," 54 percent of the non-shys replied "true," compared to only 15 percent of the love-shy men.

Two-fifths of the shy men agreed that when their mothers were angry at them, they often said and did some very strange things. Just 13 percent of the non-shy men answered in the affirmative.

Almost 45 percent of the love-shy men compared to none of the non-shy men agreed their mothers exploded into temper tantrums at them.

Some of the love-shys' mothers would bring up the subject of childbirth-related pain whenever they were angry or upset about their son's misbehavior or lack of consideration. For some of the love-shys, these maternal rages were frequent, sometimes daily occurrences. Some of the love-shy respondents spoke of their mother's temper tantrums as constituting a kind of uncontrolled fit that could last for several hours. The following quote from a 35-year-old love-shy man should provide the reader with some idea as to the truculent, ego-deflating, highly volatile, chronic irascibility that many of these women would display.

> You may find it hard to believe this. I know some of the psychiatrists I've seen have a hard time dealing with it. But from the time I was about four or five until I was about 15 or 16, my mother would have these angry fits. Oh, I guess she would have them about every ten to 14 days or so, whenever she was so angry about something that she just couldn't control herself. Well, one of the things she would do was rip off her underwear and force me to look at the scar from the excruciatingly-painful operation she said she had to have when she gave birth to me. I mean she would just rip every damn thing off in a loud and screaming rage and she'd force me to look at her pussy and this scar that she screamed was so horrendously painful. Then she'd flail her arms all over the place and start throwing silverware and coat hangers. And this would go on like for a half-hour or more sometimes. Then she'd grab this really long butcher knife we kept in the silverware drawer. And she'd show it to me, screaming at the top of her lungs. And she'd holler that she was going to commit suicide with it. And then she'd run shouting and screaming into the bathroom, and she'd lock herself in there. At that point she'd usually stop screaming. She'd just cry and cry and cry, loudly and then softly. And like I said, that would sometimes go on for three or four hours before she'd finally go to bed and sleep it off.

A 40-year old love-shy man had this to offer:

> Listen, for several years while I was growing up I don't think a single day ever went by when my mother wouldn't rant and rave about

something. She would holler at the top of her lungs, sometimes for hours, about what kind of goddam sonofabitch and rotten cur I was, and how she wished I was dead or that I'd be hit by a car or something. Then when she would come out of it she would give me all this loving bullshit about how she loved me. And she would try to stroke my head, and I just wanted to get away from her. I couldn't stand her! Even her breath stunk all the time I remember!

Now, living through one's formative years with a woman manifesting this type of capricious, highly volatile personality could well have inspired the development of generalized fear and mistrust of women in general.

Briquet's Syndrome

In listening to the love-shys discuss their mothers it became apparent to me that a large fraction of these women may have suffered from a chronic, usually life-long condition known as Briquet's Syndrome, an hysterical disorder affecting one or two percent of all women. They complain loudly about their physical difficulties even though they have no underlying physical disease. Symptoms include headache, numbness, tingling, palpitations, shortness of breath, stomach cramps, pain during coitus, painful joints and abdominal pains. Such patients often convince their exasperated physicians that genuine physical disease may lie at the root of their problems, necessitating exploratory surgery. Such surgical procedures often give rise to iatrogenesis, medical treatment, especially surgery, that itself causes medical problems.

Briquet's Syndrome women typically seek sympathy and special considerations from their families. But because their personalities are so abrasive, especially vis-a-vis their love-shy sons, they seldom enjoy much success in this regard.

Almost three-quarters of the love-shys guessed that their mothers had been shy, tense or embarrassed about being seen while pregnant compared to 11 percent of the non-shys.

Mother's Employment

Tense women are probably less likely to have long-term employment than relaxed and sociable women. Twenty to forty years ago, women were much less likely to work when pregnant. So I asked respondents if their mothers had been employed throughout most of the pregnancy, unemployed but active socially or inactive, remaining indoors most of the time. Each man had to guess at the answer. Nevertheless, the results provided confirmation for my earlier findings that mothers of love-shy men tended to be anti-social. Just 10 percent of the non-shys' mothers had been employed during pregnancy, but none of the mothers of the love-shy men had been employed during their pregnancies. Only 11 percent of the non-shy men said their mothers stayed indoors, compared to 52 percent of the younger love-shy men and 67 percent of the older love-shy men. The more severe the love-shyness, the more socially avoidant the mothers had been. As for those indicating their mother had been unemployed but active socially, the responses were 79 percent for the non-shy men, 48 percent for the younger love-shys, and 33 percent for the older love-shy men.

Employment Among Mothers of Teenagers

In addition, 77 percent of the older love-shys' mothers together with 67 percent of the mothers of the younger love-shys had never been employed at all while their children were growing up compared to 19 percent of non-shys. On the other hand, 54 percent of the non-shys' mothers had been employed full-time during this period, true for only 20 percent of the younger love-shys' mothers and for 11 percent of the mothers of the older ones.

In America we tend to be quite moralistic about mothers spending enough time with their growing children. And yet various research studies have made it clear that it is the *quality* of the time spent with children that matters, and *not* the quantity. The love-shy men quite obviously had had their mothers around quite a bit more often than the non-shy men did, not perhaps to good advantage.

Thus, maternal traits that probably affected the inborn biology of shyness also worked after birth to enhance that characteristic.

Status Consciousness

Another trait widespread among mothers of the love-shy was two-facedness. Many complained that their mothers could become different people when the telephone or door bell rang. Consider the following remark that was made by a 42-year-old love-shy man:

> There were some scenes you just wouldn't believe. My mother would be screaming and hollering and wailing at me that she wished I was dead and that I'd get hit by a car and all that. She'd be throwing glassware and books at me and yelling so loud that the neighbors at the other end of the block could hear. Then the doorbell would ring. My mother would open the door, and if it was a friend of hers she'd suddenly become a totally different person. I mean she would start laughing, and she would lovingly invite the friend in and be incredibly nice to her. This happened so many times when I was growing up. And each time I could just puke. I would just seethe inside because some of these friends of my mother would tell me how lucky I was to have such a wonderful mother. All these people would be telling me all the time my mother was just the nicest, warmest, most generous person they knew, and that I was really lucky. If I could have only told them what a vicious, poison-tongued bitch she always was, I know they'd never have believed me.

In short, you cannot tell a book by its cover. Many of these mothers were viewed by their sons as being extremely status-conscious and oriented towards creating a good impression irrespective of whatever hypocrisy or psychoemotional consequences might be involved. Deeply insecure at heart, these women simply could not permit any unpolished side of themselves to be displayed to the public.

Chapter 6

Family Composition

We can learn a great deal about the underlying causes of love-shyness by comparing the backgrounds of men who are severely afflicted with the backgrounds of men who are not. For example, if a characteristic is prevalent in the backgrounds of the non-shy men, but rare in the backgrounds of the love-shy, we might reasonably deduce that the absence of that characteristic may have some bearing on the development of severe and chronic love-shyness. Contrariwise, if a characteristic is commonplace among the love-shys and rare among the non-shys, we might similarly infer that this characteristic might have something to do with the development of love-shyness.

No characteristic or experience could, by itself, cause severe love-shyness to develop. But a number of unfortunate characteristics or experiences might influence the development of love-shyness. Each of the 500 respondents was asked to indicate the number of his brothers and sisters and their ages. The love-shys were no less likely than the non-shys to have either an older or younger brother. But there were differences concerning sisters. Only 14 percent of the self-confident men had grown up without a sister around. In contrast, 59 percent of the university-aged love-shy men had grown up without a sister, as had 71 percent of the older love-shy men. Fifty-one percent of the self-confident men grew up with two or more sisters compared to a mere four percent of the love-shy men.

Government statistics indicate that approximately one-third of all boys in the United States grow up without a sister. The non-shy men studied for this book were more self-confident than the average. Fully 86 percent or the great majority had grown up with a sister. The experience of having a sister may well have helped develop masculine self-confidence with women.

The Mode of Standardization

There is a well-supported theorem in social science called the mode of standardization stating that the more frequently two different groups interact with each other, provided that the interaction is not brought about by coercion, the better able to understand and to appreciate each other they are likely to become. Interaction also leads to increasing agreement in attitudes, values, beliefs and aspirations.

Years of interviewing very shy men have convinced me that love-shys do not understand women well emotionally. And what people do not understand they tend to fear. Men who grow up with sisters around learn to relate to girls as people who are not so different from themselves.

Important too is that sisters often bring friends home after school affording their brothers the opportunity to meet and socialize with them. During adolescence, a sister's friends can provide a pool of potential dating partners. Having a sister allows a boy to get to know girls as people whom he can joke around with, argue with, and enjoy. He learns to relax emotionally around women.

In her 1976 book, *Dilemmas of Masculinity*, Columbia University sociologist Mirra Komarovsky cited her own research evidence indicating that for young men, a history of good relations with sisters was a far more important determinant of self-confidence in successful dating and courting than was a history of good relations with brothers or even with mothers. As a case in point, almost two-thirds of the non-virginal university men in Komarovsky's study had enjoyed favorable relations with their sisters. This had been true for only two-fifths of the sexually-inexperienced university men whom she studied.

My own data indicated that neither the quality of the brother-sister relationship nor the sister's age made anywhere nearly as much difference in predicting a man's non-shyness with women as did the mere existence of a sister.

Interactions with Married People

The mode of standardization theory provides a good explanation as to why bachelors usually find married women easier to talk to than single women. Single women typically find married men easier to talk to than never-married men. Married people are used to talking to members of the opposite sex. They don't need the protective mask of a role or a script.

Despite extreme shyness, most of the men interviewed for this book could recall how relaxed the conversations they had had with married woman had been. Young women who are spontaneous and open are much easier for love-shy men to open up to than are single, never-married women who feel constrained to play a role.

One of the questions to which each of the men in this study responded reflects these problems very poignantly: "It seems whenever I develop a crush on somene I soon find out that the person is already taken." A staggering 93 percent of the love-shy men agreed with this statement compared to only 20 percent of the non-shy men. For love-shy males, the coolness of single girls caused feelings of fear, anxiety and discouragement.

The Only Child

Love-shy men were more often only children than were the self-confident group. Only seven percent of the non-shy men had grown up as only children, whereas 25 percent of the young love-shys and 31 percent of the older ones had.

The vast majority of social science research focusing on only children has found them to be better adjusted than children with siblings. This is especially true for male children, who enjoy significantly higher levels of self-esteem and social self-confidence than do the large majority of boys with brothers and sisters. They also tend to achieve higher levels of educational, vocational and financial success.

Yet this study revealed a strong relationship between only-child status and severe love-shyness. Why? My suspicion is that growing up an only child serves to increase extreme shyness only when a boy suffers from incompetent parenting and inhibition genes. My guess is that most people who have only children are at least slightly to considerably above average in parental competence. In contrast, my data strongly suggest that severely love-shy males tended to have had a history of considerably less than adequate parenting.

Thus, for those with parents of normal effectiveness, growing up as an only child can be an advantage. However, when the mother and father are less than adequately competent, the only child with the behavioral inhibition gene is left with no one around to mitigate the psychoemotional blows he often experiences. When brothers and/or sisters are around they will usually incur at least some of the parents' wrath and bizarre behavior. And even though many families with more than one child do make a scapegoat out of one specific individual (usually the least attractive or least competent child), siblings very often do protect each other to at least some extent from the behavior of hostile, capricious and bizarre parents.

With virtually no exceptions, all of the love-shy men I interviewed who had grown up as only children recounted a large number of bizarre, erratic and capricious acts by their parents, particularly their mothers. Words like "irascible," "abrasive," "truculent," "tense," "high strung," "cantankerous" and "petulant" were typically employed by this group to describe their mothers. Even as adults, few appeared to like their mothers much.

The love-shys' mothers seemed to have conveyed an extremely frightening and obnoxious image of womanhood—an image that is anything but attractive or alluring. Many of the men I interviewed had learned to accept their mother's behavior on an intellectual level, but on the deeper, emotional level, virtually none had made any headway in coming to grips with commonplace events of their formative years.

Kinship Relationships

In traditional societies, men and women were seldom left entirely to their own devices in rearing children. If a mother or a father happened to be under great stress or for some other reason could not properly care for their children, a relative, such as an aunt or an uncle, would take over for a time. In fact, even in the contemporary United States most families seem to enjoy a kinship network which provides a considerable amount of help on occasions when things become a little too tough. Recent studies on child abuse have documented the fact that physical and psychological abusers tend to be far more isolated from kin and friends than nonabusive parents. Men who beat their wives also tend to be isolated as do their victimized wives.

Accordingly, it seemed appropriate to ask both the shy and the non-shy men some questions about the extent to which other adult relatives were around, upon whom they could depend for emotional support. I asked how many could depend on three or four adults other than parents. None of the older love-shy men had anyone, and only nine percent of the young love-shys had. In contrast, an impressive 59 percent of the self-confident non-shy men could count on at least three or four adults.

Each respondent was further asked to indicate exactly how many relatives (other than parents) had been available for help and emotional support during his formative years as a child and teenager. Fully 53 percent of the non-shy men indicated that they had had three or more relatives to count on. Only eight percent of the university-aged love-shy and zero percent (nobody) of the older love-shys were able to indicate that while growing up they could count on the emotional support and encouragement of three or more adult relatives.

In fact, 87 percent of the older love-shys and 68 percent of the young ones said that there had been no relatives they could count upon. Only 27 percent of the self-confident men indicated that there had been no one they could count on.

And as for the present, 100 percent of the older love-shys and 71 percent of the young ones said that there was none they could turn to. None of the non-shys agreed.

Quality of Parents' Marriages

There is evidence that the love-shys' parents had somewhat less satisfying marriages than did the parents of the non-shys. However, the love-shys' parents were no more likely than the parents of the non-shys to have ever divorced or separated. For example, 20 percent of the non-shys' parents had either divorced or separated, 17 percent of the older love-shys and 23 percent of the younger. Looking at divorce alone, only six percent of the older love-shys' parents had been divorced, eight percent of the younger versus seven percent of the non-shys' parents. Perhaps a better barometer of marriage was to directly ask how they would rate the quality of their parents' marriage. Excluding those men whose parents had divorced, 45 percent of the older love-shys and 41 percent of the younger classified their parents' marriages as "not too happy" or "unhappy" versus 31 percent for the non-shys.

When I asked if their parents got along with each other during the childhood years or if there was conflict, fighting and dissatisfaction, only six percent of the non-shy men indicated that their parents had gotten along with each other less than moderately well. In contrast, better than one-third of the love-shys' parents were seen as having gotten along with each other less than moderately well.

I also asked: "While you were growing up, about how often did your father praise your mother?" And only 12 percent of the non-shys responded "rarely or never" compared to almost one-third of the love-shy men. This question may have some implications for the *modeling process*. Most sons, including those who do not get along very well with their fathers, model their own behavior, often unintentionally, to some extent on their fathers. The inability of love-shys to relate to young women in a positive or successful way may be partially attributable to deficits in the ways in which their own fathers treated their mothers. Because most of the love-shys' mothers were not charming or attractive, they probably didn't inspire praise or admiration from their husbands—or sons.

To be sure, generous praise had not flowed in the reverse direction either. I asked each man: "While you were growing up, about how often did your mother praise your father?" And only six percent of the non-shy men indicated "rarely or hardly ever." In contrast, almost one-third of the love-shy men indicated "rarely or hardly ever."

It appears that the love-shys' parents had significantly less emotionally satisfying marriages than those of the non-shy men. And this had doubtless been reflected in the ways the parents had behaved to each other. But it also appears that the love-shys' parents had some aversion to divorce. Perhaps there was an unhealthy, symbiotic dependency between husbands and wives in which turmoil and tension may have been perceived as less distressing than divorce.

Chapter 7

Parenting Practices and Love-Shyness

Throughout their formative years of childhood and adolescence virtually all the love-shy men studied for this book had been victims of a steady stream of psychoemotional abuse. Until just a few years ago behavioral scientists concentrated their energies on the other three major forms of child abuse: physical abuse, sexual abuse and neglect. Now, however, we know that the cumulative impact of psychoemotional abuse can be just as devastating, damaging the self-esteem of impressionable minds. Herein lies one of the major keys to the effective prevention of intractable love-shyness

Virtually all parents want the best for their children. Therefore, the spate of highly deleterious consequences resulting from child abuse are seldom if even intended. Indeed, most people intend to be better parents than their own were to them. Yet the single, best predictor of what kind of parent a given individual will be is how effective his own parents were. We tend to learn our parenting scripts from the way in which we are raised. Our early experiences tend to govern our behavior with our own children despite any intellectual ideas we may have regarding our treatment during childhood.

Persistent Belittlement and Ego-Deflation

Psychoemotional abuse usually doled out in extreme anger was the major complaint that the love-shys had against their parents. This ego-deflating hollering and screaming had been an everyday occurrence in most of the love-shys' homes. From the time they were very small children, they had to live with shouting and belittling—until they finally moved out of their parents' homes, usually to attend a university. Some of the love-shys told me they thought they had become inured to their parents' constant rantings and ravings. But since they had spent their formative years in such an unpleasant home atmosphere, a deleterious cumulative impact upon their subconscious minds seems likely.

Consider, for example, the ways in which some of the love-shys respond today to their parents' rages. Several of the men I interviewed said that they cannot stop from breaking into uncontrolled hysterical laughter whenever one of their parents displays a temper tantrum. Others simply escape the situation by shutting themselves in their bedrooms until the tantrum subsides. Still others admit they become depressed whenever they have to listen to their parents rant and rave.

Even the older love-shys occasionally visit their aging parents, but the parents seldom or never visit them. The non-shy young men were visited by their parents on average five times more frequently than the love-shys.

Curiously, some level of partial financial dependence appeared to be a major motive for many of these visits. Some of the love-shys continue even in their 30s and 40s to receive some level of financial support from their parents. The love-shys would visit their parents' home and receive money along with heavy doses of angry, psychoemotional abuse. Some of these love-shys figure that the abuse was simply the price they had to pay for the money they were getting. Some of the fathers did not like the way their love-shy sons were dressing or the sort of employment (many were under-employed). Many of the fathers continued to be very disappointed and upset about their adult sons' lack of competitive masculine drive. But paradoxically, while the fathers were berating their love-shy sons for holding menial, deadend jobs, for dressing shabbily and for not settling down and raising a family, they would simultaneously give them money.

Most of the love-shys' parents probably did what they thought was best for their sons. I suspect that many of them felt hurt by their sons' non-masculine behavior and intractable, seemingly deliberate unwillingness to behave as real boys should. The more refractory the sons became, the more exasperated, hurt and enraged the parents became. All people like to have control over their lives. The love-shys' behavior tended to make their parents feel powerless, a very painful and emotionally-disconcerting way for anyone to feel.

Of course, a central part of the problem was that the parents wanted their sons to make changes that were impossible for them. Constant haranguing just made matters worse, estranging parent from child.

A child must feel accepted and loved as he is before he can work on changing himself. For a child to feel love, that love must be freely given with a genuine sensitivity to and compassion for the needs, wants and feelings of the loved one. Feeling loved is of infinitely greater importance for a child's well-being and future socio-emotional growth than is simply being loved. Even if all pre-love-shy boys had felt loved, they would not have developed into highly energetic, aggressive, outgoing adults. But feeling loved, I believe, would have prevented highly-sensitive children from becoming love-shy, unhappy and poorly adjusted adults.

Anger and Rage

Anger and rage are commonly understood by psychologists as responses to being emotionally hurt and made to feel unimportant. People tend to be less courteous toward members of their own immediate family than to friends or strangers. They also tend to be less courteous to their own children than to other people's children.

The love-shy men remembered their parents as having bad tempers. For example, 53 percent of the older love-shy men and 47 percent of the younger ones said their mothers were easily angered and prone to temper outbursts versus 20 percent of the non-shys. Further, 41 percent of the older love-shys and 36 percent of the younger ones said their fathers were easily angered contrasted with 21 percent of the non-shys.

Forty-five percent of the older love-shys and 39 percent of the younger ones indicated that their mothers often threw uncontrollable temper tantrums, while this was true for none of the non-shy men. Whereas 73 percent of the non-shys indicated their mothers never threw tantrums, 30 percent of the older love-shys and 39 percent of the younger ones told me that it had never happened.

Parental swearing was another unattractive memory. In response to the statement: "When I was a child my father would very often swear, holler and cuss at me," 40 percent of the older love-shys and 35 percent of the younger ones indicated "true," compared to only 14 percent of the non-shy men. Forty-eight percent of the older love-shys and 37 percent of the younger said their mothers cussed at them versus only six percent for the non-shys.

And in response to the statement: "My mother would often scream that she wished I would die or that I was dead," fully 38 percent of the older love-shys and 30 percent of the younger ones indicated that this had happened on several occasions. Only three percent of the non-shys indicated that it had ever happened to them. As a case in point, a 23-year-old love-shy recounted the following:

> Oh, every time I go home for a holiday my mother turns really rabid after a few days. She does things like screaming that she can't understand why so many nice kids get killed in automobile accidents and plane crashes while a dirty rotten sonofabitch like me is permitted to live. Ha! Ha! Ha! I mean, she always really screams that! Last time I was back there she asked me point blank—why don't I just take my car and crash it into a tree somewhere at 90 miles an hour! She says I'd be doing her and the rest of society a favor and that I wouldn't have to suffer anymore either.

Spankings, Beatings, and Physical Abuse

Despite the fact that psychoemotional abuse was the major theme as far as the family backgrounds of the love-shys were concerned, physical assaults on the love-shys were also common-place, accompanied by loud shouting, screaming and abusive hol-lering. Twenty-two percent of the self-confident, non-shy men claimed that their parents had never used corporal punishment. This was true for none among the love-shys. More specifically, 21 percent of the non-shys had been spanked or beaten on an average of at least once or more every ten days during childhood, while 44 percent of the younger love-shys and 58 percent of the older ones had suffered the same treatment.

Better than three-quarters of all parents had relied on their bare hands most of the time. However, 82 percent of the love-shys' parents had relied heavily upon the use of belts, whereas 56 percent of the non-shys' parents had only occasionally used belts. Nineteen percent of the love-shys' parents had occasionally used razor straps; none of the non-shys mentioned razor straps. On the other hand, 14 percent of the non-shys' parents had occasionally used hair-brushes, compared to 21 percent of the parents of the love-shys. Straps were mentioned by 62 percent of the love-shys, compared to just 31 percent of the non-shys. Wooden rulers were used occasionally by 39 percent of the love-shys' parents, compared to just 15 percent of the non-shys' parents. Sticks or birch rods were mentioned by 38 percent of the love-shys, compared to just seven percent of the non-shys. And whereas none of the non-shys claimed to have ever been beaten with heavy wooden paddle boards, these were mentioned by 33 percent of the love-shy men. Dog leashes were similarly mentioned by 19 percent of the love-shys, but by none of the non-shys. And 12 percent of the love-shys had been beaten with wooden coat hangers; none of the non-shys had ever been beaten with same.

Perhaps the major difference between the love-shys and the non-shys is that corporal punishment was an integral part of the normal way of life in at least half of the love-shys' homes. This was true for little more than one-fifth of the non-shys' homes. The love-shys' parents were a good deal more likely than the non-shys' to respond to frustration, annoyance and wrongdoing in a physical manner. It would thus appear that the love-shys had grown up with parents who had above average difficulty with impulse control.

Another major difference between the homes of the love-shys

and those of the non-shys is that the mother tended to be the major source of discipline. In fact, 47 percent of the older love-shys and 38 percent of the younger ones agreed that the mother had done mostly all of the punishment. Contrariwise, this had been true for only six percent of the non-shy men.

On the basis of these differences, it seems quite possible that the mothers' basic nature and behavioral style may have helped significantly to set the stage for the love-shys' strong fears concerning informal social interaction vis-a-vis women, and their basic, underlying nervousness. Experimental psychology has clearly taught us that introverts and low-anxiety threshold people condition responses much faster and more deeply than extroverts. Living on a day-to-day basis with an enormously high-strung woman certainly could not have done anything positive in terms of promoting a relaxed, easy-going ability to relate in a friendly manner with women.

Finally, I asked each respondent to indicate how old he had been the last or most recent time one of his parents had inflicted any physical punishment on him. And the differences between the three groups of research respondents were quite substantial. The average age for the cessation of corporal punishment for the non-shy men was 11.6. For the young love-shy men the average age had been 15.9. The average age when the older love-shys had stopped receiving corporal punishment was 17.2.

Family Emotional Supportiveness

I asked each man: "To what extent did you feel that your parents believed in you and supported you emotionally?" And 67 percent of the non-shy men answered "a great deal," compared to only 32 percent of the younger love-shys and 23 percent of the older ones. In contrast, 58 percent of the older love-shy men felt that their parents had provided them with very little if any emotional support. Among the younger love-shys, 48 percent felt that they had received very little if any emotional support compared to a mere 13 percent of the non-shy men.

Meaningful participation by children in dinner-table conversation has been found by a good many researchers to correlate highly with active participation as adults in community and political affairs. Thus, I asked each respondent how frequently he participated meaningfully in dinner-table conversation during his formative years. The differences between the love-shys and the non-shys were substantial. For example, 80 percent of the non-shy men indicated that their participation in dinner-table conversation had been frequent or very frequent, compared to only 36 percent of the younger love-shys and just 23 percent of the older love-shys.

It is not surprising that there were rather substantial differences between the three groups with regard to their ease in discussing their problems with their parents. Whereas 52 percent of the non-shys felt easy, only 17 percent of the younger love-shys and 10 percent of the older love-shys felt the same way. Indeed, 66 percent of the older love-shys and 57 percent of the younger ones felt quite the opposite, while only 19 percent of the non-shys felt that way.

The love-shys' parents evidently had not acted particularly interested in what their sons had had to say. Fifty-two percent of the older love-shys and 45 percent of the younger ones said their parents were either not too interested or not interested, while none of the non-shys believed that to be true. In fact, 74 percent of the non-shy men indicated that their parents had been interested in them.

And when I asked: "How frequently did you enjoy informal conversations with your mother about any topic?" only five percent of the non-shy men indicated infrequently. In contrast, 58 percent of the older love-shys together with 46 percent of the younger ones indicated that they had enjoyed such conversations on an infrequent basis. The findings when this same question was asked in regard to fathers were similar. Forty-three percent of the older love-shys and 37 percent of the younger ones indicated that they had enjoyed informal conversations with their fathers on an infrequent basis. None of the non-shy men agreed.

Another question pertinent to parental emotional supportiveness which clearly differentiated the three different groups of respondents was: "When you received a low grade at school on a test or paper, did you feel free and comfortable about discussing the matter with your mother?" Fully 65 percent of the non-shy men indicated the affirmative, compared to only 39 percent of the younger love-shy, and just 32 percent of the older love-shys. Perhaps most revealing of all, 43 percent of the older love-shys and 35 percent of the younger ones believed their mothers sometimes acted as though they didn't exist. None of the non-shy men thought this was true.

I asked the same question with regard to fathers, and was somewhat surprised to find a somewhat less pathological set of responses than I found with regard to the mothers. Only 30 percent of the older love-shys and 22 percent of the younger felt that their fathers had sometimes acted as though they did not exist. Again, none of the non-shys felt that their fathers had ever ignored their existence.

Family Democracy

The issue of family democracy is obviously quite closely related to how open and spontaneous family communication had been. A democratic family environment is one in which children play an active role in making and revising rules, regulations and policies that impact upon them. It is an environment characterized by high levels of mutual respect, mutual trust and love. The parents in such families intuitively realize that they are the ones who must inspire respect, love and trust.

To gauge the degree of democracy, I asked how much influence respondents had in making and revising family rules and policies that affected them. Eighty-two percent of the older love-shy men and 69 percent of the younger love-shys had little or no influence over the way their families had been managed, compared to only 26 percent of the non-shy men. Putting it another way, 74 percent of the non-shys had had either much or some influence over the ways their families had been managed, compared to only 18 percent of the older love-shys and 31 percent of the younger love-shys.

Later on in the interview, to assure reliability, I asked each man to react to this statement: "While I was growing up, even though I was a child I usually had a meaningful role in the way our family was run." Fully 73 percent of the non-shy men answered true to this statement, compared to only 34 percent of the younger love-shys and 27 percent of the older ones.

Mutual Sensitivity to Needs and Feelings

The study clearly indicated that the parents, especially the mothers, of love-shy men did little to make their sons feel loved. In addition, they had very little if any awareness or insight into the way their behavior and words were affecting their sons' psychoemotional development. This lack of insight and sensitivity is the very essence of chronic psychological abuse. A 24-year-old man describes what it was like:

> Ah, she had the radio or the television on all the time. If I came in the room where she was, she'd scream at me that she was trying to concentrate. Even during meal times she would have the radio on. I can remember throughout all my school years how my mother and my father would both clobber me if I opened my mouth while we were eating dinner. They wanted to concentrate on what some news commentator was saying. And when I grew older, it was the same old story, even if the program was some stupid contest show or soap opera. Everything was more important than I was. I guess at the time I didn't think of it that way. But as I grew older I began to realize that I was just sort of a distraction to my parents. I was never the main show, or even the cartoon for that matter.

Most of the love-shys' mothers undoubtedly believed that they truly loved their sons. In fact, many of these mothers frequently screamed out that they loved their sons. But they didn't show it, and their sons certainly never felt it. They might say one thing but do something that conveyed an entirely different message.

Many parents were preoccupied with shaping and molding their sons to enhance their own status and prestige. They cared that their sons would fit their image of what a good son should be like. But they did not care about their sons as people with deep feelings, emotions, needs and wants requiring recognition, respect and emotional support.

There is an interesting paradox here. Many of the love-shys' parents were quite generous, giving their sons material things but then complaining how ungrateful they were. The following interview with a 20-year-old illustrates this:

> Oh, my parents were generous alright! The trouble is they were usually generous with the wrong things. Like even when I was a young kid my parents would constantly drag me into the best clothing stores. I was always the best dressed kid in town. They would constantly buy all these expensive outfits for me. But when I asked them to buy me a toy or a book or a record album on the way home, they would complain about how spoiled I was. And they would threaten to beat the shit out of me if I didn't stop agitating them about a toy. They were always very generous about getting me what I didn't particularly want or care about. But when it came to something I really did want, the answer was always how spoiled and ungrateful I was, and why I didn't get the hell out and earn the money to buy it myself. The strange thing is—what they were buying me always cost a great deal more money than the things I really did want. And some of the things they bought I seldom even wore.

The preoccupation that many of the love-shys' parents had about clothing and appearance is reflected in the response to this statement: "Until I graduated from high school, my parents almost always decided what I would wear each day." Thirty-three percent of the older love-shys and 22 percent of the younger love-shys agreed with this statement compared to none of the non-shy men.

One love-shy man spontaneously volunteered that every morning until the day he graduated from high school his father would come into his bedroom, drag him up, put his socks on for him and then physically drag him into the bathroom where he would wash the son's face and remove in a sometimes painful manner any blackheads which had been apparent. And while the father did all this he would angrily berate his son for being irresponsible and uncaring about being late for school.

Milk versus Honey

In his celebrated 1956 work entitled *The Art of Loving*, social philosopher Erich Fromm distinguished between two types of love:

milk and honey. Milk has to do with providing a child with food, clothing, shelter and luxuries. Honey, on the other hand, has to do with conveying to the child a sense of deep personal worth, happiness, vibrancy—a feeling that life itself is intrinsically rich and highly worthwhile.

When people lack self-confidence, they often develop a preoccupation with appearances. Highly-tense and less-than-happy parents often shower their children with all manner of material goodies—milk, to use Fromm's metaphorical term. When the recipients do not respond in the expected manner, parents are likely to angrily accuse them of being ungrateful, spoiled, and inconsiderate. Yet these frustrated parents persist in showering their ungrateful children with more and more milk.

Yet some children receive a surfeit of milk and grow up to be a joy both to themselves and to their parents. What makes a difference is the presence of a significant amount of honey along with the milk.

Virtually hundreds of research studies have shown that if a parent is effective at providing honey—if the child really enjoys being with his parents—the amount of influence the parents wield is great. This is because the child has not erected any defensive barriers against the parents. The child automatically internalizes his parents' values without being aware that he is doing so.

Parents cannot own a child the way they own material possessions. Children are independent souls who are in their parents' charge for a very brief time. The most successful parent-child relationships, like the most successful and happy husband-wife relationships, are those where there is mutual respect and where all parties are accepted for what they are and are free to be themselves. Only when a person is accepted, is he free to grow and to change.

The love-shys' parents could not accept their sons as their sons actually were but kept trying to change them. They could not relax and enjoy their children, a key prerequisite for providing the necessary honey.

But more importantly, not accepting a child as he is will almost always cause that child to erect an impenetrable, defensive wall around himself. The child thus develops a vested interest in sustaining his highly-criticized behavior patterns, including the ones that are self-defeating. Under these circumstances meaningful parent-child communication becomes impossible. And what started out as biologically-rooted behavior inhibition is catalyzed into becoming an increasingly intractable case of severe and chronic shyness.

As New York University psychiatrists Alexander Thomas and Stella Chess have convincingly demonstrated, inborn behavioral inhibition need not give rise to lifelong social isolation and intractable shyness. When the parents of such children are trained to be encouraging and genuinely accepting and to exude a relaxed feeling of confidence in their child's worth and potential (together with a feeling of confident expectancy that things will go well), the children tend to flourish. Inborn behavioral inhibition need not doom a child. It is the way that parents react to inborn behavioral inhibition that makes the difference.

Chapter 8

How the All-Male Peer Group
Creates Shy Men

Love-shy men learn very early in life to associate feelings of fear, anxiety and physical pain with the idea of informal interaction in all-male peer groups. Most human beings, on the other hand, look forward with enthusiasm to socializing with their peers. Being placed in solitary confinement has long been recognized as one of the most cruel and extreme of all punishments.

Over the years, psychologists have repeatedly showed that the most important predictor of happiness is satisfaction with informal friendships. Since most of us associate friendly peer-group interaction with feelings of pleasure, it is highly significant that the love-shy associate the idea of male peers with pain, fear and anxiety. Indeed, the very idea of associating with a group of males conjures up such displeasure that the love-shy take special pains to avoid peers. The love-shy, then, often deliberately choose a life of solitary confinement. It is important to understand why these people build their own defensive prison walls. Armed with this knowledge, it may be possible to engineer an elementary school environment that deters shy children from building insurmountable walls around themselves.

The peer group is of enormous importance in ensuring healthy growth and development. This appears to be especially true for males. There is evidence that the same-sexed peer group is of considerably less importance for females. For example, women who are unpopular with their own sex, often become highly popular with men, but males unpopular with members of their own sex virtually never become popular or even mildly successful with women. The social requirement that males must be the ones to initiate contact with women may partially account for this. Reputation may be another important consideration. Our cultural norms require males to impress females with their social/economic competence, not vice versa. The all-male peer group can provide a great boost to positive self-esteem and social self-confidence.

Males without a network of male friends have nothing to support them in their natural strivings to become assertive in a positive, friendly way vis-a-vis potentially eligible female dating partners. Simply put, a reasonable level of success within the all-male peer group constitutes a prime prerequisite for a male's ability to attain even a very mild degree of success in securing female companionship.

The Key Importance for Dating of Friendship Networks

During the past decade sociologists have published numerous research studies which have highlighted the importance of informal friendship networks. One of the key findings is that most Americans meet their future spouses through their friends. Popular folklore would have us believe that Cupid accomplishes most of his work at beaches, bars, discotheques, zoos, bus stops, or at work. But informal friendship networks actually instigate far more male-female relationships that eventually lead to premarital cohabitation and/or marriage. Even the best jobs are secured some 70 percent of the time through informal social networks. Love and work, the two most crucial ingredients of our lives, both depend on quality friendships. The more solid our friendship networks are, the more solid will be our satisfactions and reward in love and work.

It is easier to meet members of the opposite sex through

friendship networks than through any other means. It requires more social self-confidence to initiate a conversation with a total stranger than it does with someone to whom one has been introduced by a mutual friend. If this is true for the vast majority, it is certainly true for shy people.

Severe shyness prevents a person from immersing himself in social networks. So he is forced to deal with impersonal agencies and meeting places if he ever hopes to find a wife.

How the All Male Peer Group Creates Shy Men

Through their lives the love-shys had experienced significantly fewer friendships than had the non-shys, and the few friendships that a minority of them had experienced had been very shallow. In fact, most of the love-shy men I interviewed had been social isolates throughout most of their lives.

For example, I asked each man: "When you were growing up, how many people close to your own age and whom you felt free to contact, did you have readily available to you to help you deal with school and the various other problems and anxieties associated with growing up?" The differences in the pattern of responses between the three groups of men were quite substantial.

Thus, 83 percent of the older love-shy men and 65 percent of the younger love-shys indicated that they had had no one. In contrast, this had been the case for none of the self-confident men. In fact, 57 percent of the non-shys indicated that they had had at least three or more close friends throughout their formative years. Only 11 percent of the younger love-shys and none of the older love-shys could say that they had had three or more close friends throughout the duration of their formative years. In addition, 73 percent of the older love-shys and 53 percent of the younger ones agreed with the more extreme statement that they never had any friends. Nobody among the non-shys agreed with that statement.

In order to tap the level of satisfaction each respondent felt with his current situation, I simply asked the following: "In general, do you feel that you have as many friends of the various kinds as you would like?" And 94 percent of the non-shy men indicated "yes," compared to a mere eight percent of the younger love-shys and zero percent of the older love-shys.

This social distance which the love-shy feel from the human race apparently extends even to relatives and kin. I asked each man: "How many relatives do you see often and consider close friends?" And 84 percent of the older love-shys together with 68 percent of the younger ones said "none," compared to just 26 percent of the self-confident non-shys. In contrast, 45 percent of the non-shys saw four or more relatives often and considered them close friends. This was the case for none of the love-shy men.

The Harlow Research

In his work with rhesus monkeys, University of Wisconsin primatologist Harry Harlow found that young animals deprived of play were incapable of having sex as adults. Peer-group-deprived female monkeys would not allow even socially-successful male monkeys to mount them. These sexually-disinterested females had to be impregnated by artificial insemination. On giving birth, they tended to treat their young as feces. They stomped on it, threw it against cage walls, ignored it and in some cases actually started eating it.

The male monkeys deprived of a peer group while growing up tended to sit in a corner and simply stare at the females. Harlow placed deprived males in enclosures with sexually-receptive females. In spite of the favorable gender-ratio and lack of sexual competition, these males refused to make any efforts to mount females. Indeed, most of these deprived male monkeys didn't even play with the females. In most cases they simply sat on the sidelines watching and staring.

A particularly interesting point regarding these findings is that the "watching and staring" reaction of the deprived male monkeys seems to be very commonplace among love-shy human males. In essence, rather than risk making an approach, love-shy human males quite commonly just simply watch and stare and daydream. Even when there are six women to every man, the love-shy male still just stares.

As Harlow was able to demonstrate, play and related childhood experiences constitute a crucial preparation for adult roles. And so it is with human children. To the extent that a person is deprived of play with other children, he will grow up inadequately prepared to fulfill adult family and employment roles.

W.I. Thomas and Florian Znaniecki, in their book, *The Polish Peasant in America,* cite many cases of Polish-American boys who had been severely mistreated by their parents. Most of these impoverished boys responded to such insensitive treatment by developing a strong sense of solidarity with their male peers. Those who remained well-integrated members of peer networks became effective, well adjusted adults. The few who lacked a friendship group to turn to in times of severe stress and unfair treatment tended to become isolated and very poorly-functioning adults.

Thomas and Znaniecki's conclusions regarding human children are very smilar to those arrived at by Harlow in his work with rhesus monkeys. In essence, Harlow found that young monkeys could almost always be expected to survive ineffective mothering if they had had the benefit of young monkey playmates.

As scores of social scientists have demonstrated, children who do not experience a childhood become very poorly adjusted adults. A person's *social* adjustment as an adult is directly related to his having been actively involved in social play as a child. Child's play is important, especially to the extent that it involves cooperative, friendly interaction with a network of age-mate peers.

At one point in the interviews, I asked each respondent to react to the statement: "I guess I was never really a child." The results backed up the traditional wisdom about the importance of childhood. None of the self-confident non-shys agreed with this statement. In contrast, fully 71 percent of the older love-shys and 59 percent of the younger love-shys saw fit to agree with it.

Bullying

Love-shy males learn early in life to perceive peer interaction as painful. If this is indeed the case, socially-avoidant behavior along with self-imposed social isolation becomes more easily understandable.

The male peer group among elementary-school-aged boys can be extremely cruel. The reasons why have been given far too little attention by researchers. There are scores of societies all over the world in which violence, cruelty and bullying, including psychological hazing, are absent from children's peer groups.

I asked each of my respondents to react to the statement: "When I was a child I was often bullied by other children of my own age." It is important to note that none of the 200 non-shys indicated that this had been true. In stark contrast, fully 94 percent of the older love-shys together with 81 percent of the younger love-shys indicated that the statement was true. In essence, better than four-fifths of even the younger shy men had been frequently bullied while growing up. For the older love-shys almost all had been frequently bullied.

Doubtless the physical and psychoemotional hazing interacted with a "weak" native temperament in a synergistic kind of way. Undoubtedly, the net result of this was to enhance the inborn behavioral inhibition and the consequent social avoidance tendencies of these children. Because of low inborn anxiety and emotional sensitivity thresholds, the love-shy men probably suffered far more psychoemotional pain and scarring than a non-shy person would have suffered even if such a non-shy person had been the recipient of the same quantity of bullying and psychoemotional hazing. Bullies like to select victims whose displeasure and suffering is clearly evident for all to see and perversely enjoy. Fully 94 percent of the older love-shy men had never fought back as children. Among the younger love-shys, 77 percent had not. In contrast, only 18 percent of the non-shy men indicated that they had never fought back. And several of these men added that it had never been necessary for them to do so because no one had ever punched them in the first place. Even at the senior high school level the love-shy men had suffered a lot of bullying and psychoemotional harassment, true for none of the non-shy men.

A very good case can be made for the proposition that love-shy heterosexuals ought not be expected to play at all in the company of high-energy aggressive extroverts. In April 1985, the

New York City school district opened up the nation's first high school for homosexuals and lesbians, Harvey Milk High School. A key raison d'etre was that such children could not learn effectively in regular high schools with all the bullying and psychoemotional harassment to which they had been subjected.

I would suggest that behaviorally inhibited, emotionally sensitive boys (pre-love-shy heterosexuals) are up against essentially the same problem. As such, special coeducational facilities might well be expected to bring the best out of such temperamentally-handicapped children. Under conditions of a strong self-esteem a person can far more readily contribute the most to his own well-being and that of his community.

Frailness of Body Build

In addition to having a sensitive temperament, love-shys often were of frail build, another element contributing to unpopularity. Young boys are constantly being programmed by their parents and by the mass media to admire physical strength and daring, and to detest, and even punish, physical weakness and fearfulness.

Because of the biases in American all-male peer group culture which reward the strong and punish the weak, I asked each man to respond to the following: "Comparing yourself to other students of your size, weight, and sex when you were in high school, how physically strong or weak were you?"

Sixty-six percent of the older love-shys and 42 percent of the younger ones perceived themselves as having been physically weaker than most of their male contemporaries, in contrast to only nine percent of the non-shys. In fact, 55 percent of the non-shys believed that they had been stronger than most of their contemporaries. Only 21 percent of the younger love-shys and just four percent of the older ones felt that they had been physically stronger than most of their age-mates. The remaining men indicated that they had been "about equally as strong as most others."

First Impressions

First impressions can be lasting. Often they set the stage for a person's future orientations toward a particular person or situation.

This would certainly appear to be the case as far as the all-male peer group is concerned. The following remarks by a 20-year-old are representative:

> Before I started school I don't remember ever being lonely. I usually had companions, but they were usually girls. I didn't think anything of it actually. There was this one little girl I used to play with all the time when I was three and four years old. In fact, I guess I played with her until we were both about ready to start school. She was the same age as I was, and we enjoyed being together. But our mothers were beginning to get rather nervous that we should be with kids of our own sex. I know my mother was really nervous about my being with ths girl all the time. So one day about a week before I was supposed to start kindergarten she takes me to this house a few blocks from where we lived. And I remember there were a lot of boys my age there. I remember they were running around on the lawn, screaming at each other and knocking each other down. One of the kids had a football, and he threw it at me hard. I was just standing there with my mother, and I practically shit in my pants! She was pushing me to join in, and she was saying things like "Doesn't that look like fun!" and "Isn't that fun?" and "Why don't you run after them and join in?" and "See, Billy is here! Why don't you join him?"
>
> Well, I was just five years old at the time. And I had never known fear before. But boy! I really felt fear watching these kids! In retrospect, I guess what really bothered me was this idea that what I was watching was supposed to be fun! Jesus! I mean I might just as well have been watching a pack of wild tigers at play! I mean it was like I was watching a totally different species of animal! That's how detached I felt. Even though I was only five I realized right then and there that I was a different breed of animal than these kids I was watching. And I didn't know how to convey to my mother that this stuff they were doing didn't look anything like what I believed to be fun! My mother started to get really angry that I didn't want to join in. And it took several of the other mothers there to convince her not to force me—that I wasn't ready.
>
> And I wasn't holding on to my mother's hand either. Even at that age I wasn't comfortable with my mother. I remember I reacted by backing farther and farther away from both my mother and the kids who were kicking each other and knocking one another down. I just wanted to go off by myself and find my girlfriend to play with.

Actually I was looking forward to starting school because I thought the kids at school would play nicely—you know, games like hide-and-seek, and hopscotch, and other games I played with my girlfriend. When I finally did start school I realized the very opposite was true. And I became more and more envious of the girls with each passing day because I felt I belonged with them. They were doing the things I liked to do while every minute with the boys was like bloody hell.

All children should not be forced into the same mold. I believe that chronic love-shyness and the lifetime of loneliness and social isolation that it brings are part of the price that is intrinsic in this traditional and unchallenged way of trying to channel children.

As a case in point, each of my respondents was asked to react to the following statement: "When I was six or seven years old, just watching boys partake in 'rough and tumble' type play activities scared me to death. I resented any expectation that I try to join in. I wanted just one or two close friends who would play gently and with no chance of anyone getting knocked down or hurt in any way." Among the older love-shy men, fully 79 percent indicated agreement with this statement, while 67 percent of the younger ones agreed. In contrast, none of the self-confident felt that way.

In a related question, I asked for reactions to the statement: "When I was a child in elementary school, being knocked down by one of my peers was one of my greatest fears." And here again, fully 87 percent of the older love-shy men and 73 percent of the younger love-shys indicated "yes, this was true." In contrast, only 19 percent of the non-shys said that the statement held any truth for themselves.

These data suggest that there is a strong relationship between the degree of fear experienced in all-male peer groups and the severity of love-shyness as adults.

If we create options for children and afford them a choice of peer group, we are likely to observe a sharp diminution in the incidence of incipient neuroticism, homosexuality, as well as love-shyness.

The Baseball, Basketball and Football Syndrome

So deeply imbedded is the triumvirate of contact sports—football, basketball, and baseball—in our concept of masculinity that some young fathers-to-be erect basketball hoops as soon as they learn that their wives are bearing a male fetus. People expect a boy's interest to immediately perk up as soon as they hear the words baseball or football. They often react with amazement when these words do not arouse an enthusiastic response.

Because of these societal expectations, I asked each respondent a collection of questions about his attitudes during childhood towards a variety of sports. For example, I asked: "When you were growing up, how much did you like to play football?" And not surprisingly, zero percent of the older love-shys and only seven percent of the younger ones indicated that they had loved to play it, in contrast to 73 percent of the non-shy men. On the other hand, none of the non-shys disliked playing football, versus 89 percent of the younger love-shys and fully 100 percent of the older ones.

Given a choice between touch football and bowling, 87 percent of the non-shys selected touch football, while none of the older love-shys, and just nine percent of the younger love-shys chose it.

In a related question, I asked: "Supposing you were at an all day picnic as a 15-year-old. Suppose one group composed only of boys your own age was going to play games such as football, baseball and basketball all day long. The other group would spend the day learning how to play golf and would be composed of eight boys and eight girls. Which group do you think you would have been more likely to have selected?" Quite interestingly, only 52 percent of the non-shy men selected the baseball, basketball and football over the coeducational golf group. All 100 percent of the older love-shys and 98 percent of the younger love-shys similarly selected the coeducational golf-learning option.

These findings suggest that many naturally assertive boys might prefer more gentle pursuits, such as golf. Since golf can be played throughout one's life and offers good outdoor exercise, there is no reason why it and other non-contact sports should not be an option for school children who want nothing to do with baseball, basketball and football.

The national pastime fared little better among the love-shys than did football. Only four percent of the older love-shys and 13 percent of the younger ones had any enthusiasm for baseball as they were growing up compared to 86 percent of the non-shy men.

Given a choice between tennis and baseball, 66 percent of the non-shys opted for the baseball, versus none of the older love-shys and just five percent of the younger ones.

Love-shy men tend to view basketball with almost as much trepidation as they view football and baseball. Several of the men I interviewed commented on the flailing hands and arms and the speed of the game. Some were afraid of getting their eyes or teeth hurt while others felt they lacked sufficient coordination to handle the speed. During high school, 95 percent of the older love-shys and 82 percent of the younger ones had preferred volleyball to basketball, versus 27 percent of the non-shy men.

The "Left Out" Syndrome

One love-shy man told me that when his elementary school teachers required him to go outside and play baseball the kids assigned him to play the position of "left out" even though he actually wanted to play. Whether they wanted to be involved in sports or not, a strong message was sent to the love-shys time and again. "Get out of here! We don't want you! We don't need you! You're no good!" Often a gym teacher had to force children to pick the shys for their team. Ninety-one percent of the older love-shys and 70 percent of the younger ones said they were usually last to be chosen for team sports compared to three percent of the non-shys. In fact, whereas only one percent of the non-shys were assigned the position of "left out" in elementary school, 86 percent of the older love-shys and 62 percent of the younger ones suffered the indignity.

This sort of experience repeated time and again throughout the formative years would drastically lower a child's self-esteem. It teaches him to fear playing with peers and to look for pleasure in solitary pursuits rather than sociable ones. Many educators strongly believe that team sports teach children how to get along with each other, but evidence indicates that inhibited boys are harmed rather than helped by such sports. All children need exercise, but they do not all require the same type. Forcing sensitive boys to play games they don't like makes them despise exercise. And in avoiding exercise, they are also avoiding the opportunities for the development of social self-confidence and interpersonal skills. They become social isolates.

Almost all sports, including such gentle ones as ping pong, volleyball and shuffle board, require at least one partner. In order to have a partner one must have a friend. And in order to sustain a friendship, one must have a certain minimum of social self-confidence. The socially isolated, behaviorally inhibited adult usually does not participate in any sport because he simply has no one with whom to play.

Options must be made available to all school children so that assertive boys can happily pursue football, while shy boys can enjoy volleyball, lawn bowling, miniature golf, ping pong or swimming. And they must have the right to enjoy these activities with girls in a coeducational setting.

It cannot be emphasized too strongly that socially-withdrawn boys typically feel out of place in all-male groups. Whenever they are placed in such groups, they generally fantasize about being with girls anyway. Lacking sisters as many of them do, they desperately need to learn how to interact comfortably with girls and to engage in mutually enjoyable small talk. Hence, it is best that all of their required physical education be coeducational.

Current Peer-Group Interaction

At the time they were interviewed, virtually none of the 300 love-shy men were involved with any significant friendships. A small number of them carried on a semi-active letter writing correspondence with pen pals around the world. Some occasionally received invitations from co-workers to attend informal get-togethers. But none had anyone of either gender whom they felt free to call up, visit or go to a movie or a restaurant with. In fact, none of these men had any kind of informal friendship network.

Most of these men had surprisingly good insight into how during their formative years they had learned to associate peer interaction with pain and humiliation. In fact, many of them were too introspective. Not having any friends to distract them, many would typically spend a great deal of time each day brooding about the past and the influence that it might have had upon them. Often such brooding would be interrupted only by their listening to their stereos or watching television.

Discrepancy Between the Actual Self and the Ideal Self

The idea of having a girlfriend was central to both the value system and emotional health of every love-shy man I studied. In order for a person to appear genuine, to converse spontaneously without sham or pretense, that person's lifestyle must reflect some of the things he thinks about all the time, the things that are important to him.

In order for a love-shy man to have a male friend, he must first be actively involved in a romantic love relationship with a woman so that he can have something real to talk about. Conversation in a friendship can't just be based on dreams. An interview with a 24-year-old man contains useful insights:

> Well, I've given a lot of thought to the idea of male friendships. I suppose it would be nice. I mean, it might help me. See, if I were going with someone (a girl) it would be just so damned much easier for me to have male friends. I'd have something to talk about with them. But right now, what the hell would I talk about with a male friend? I mean, everything I think about concerns a woman! And I haven't got one! If I ever found a male friend who was anything like me, it would make me even more depressed because he wouldn't be able to help me. The guys I would really like to have as friends—I mean the guys who are engaged or going with someone—well, they're not interested in having me as a friend. Like at work, some of those guys think I'm a homo. They don't think I have anything in common with them—which is ridiculous because I bet I do a lot more thinking and dreaming about women than any of them do!

A 23-year-old told me:

This may sound stupid. But I don't feel as though I'm the real me! Like I sometimes feel totally detached from the person I am because the person I am is not able to do the things that are really important to the real me. It's like the person that I am manifesting behaviorally is a total stranger to the real me, the me that includes the things in life that are really important to me. I have no control over the person I'm presenting to the world because my anxieties prevent me from doing the things I would really like to do. If I had any male friends how would I be able to maintain a straight face with them? I mean, what I would want to talk about with them and how I actually behave in real life are two drastically different things. I'd be seen as a hypocrite. The type of male friend I'd like to have would be bored with me because I wouldn't have anything to offer him. I wouldn't even have the nerve to confess my extremely strong desire to have a woman to love.

How can the love-shy be expected to cultivate and develop male friendships when all they ever think about is women and their deprivation of same?

In order for a love-shy to have male friendships he must develop a reasonable degree of harmony between the deeply held values and interests of his ideal self and his real self. A real self that is at drastic variance with the ideal effectively blocks spontaneous communication. In addition, it makes the love-shy man appear bored and disinterested in what the other men are talking about. He appears self-centered and self-preoccupied.

Chapter 9

Preadolescent Love and Infatuation

There is a strange and curious paradox in the backgrounds of the love-shy. Since they are constantly without female companionship, others view them as being "disinterested" or as being "extremely late starters." Yet the love-shy men who were studied had actually become intensely, romantically interested in the opposite sex significantly earlier in life than had the non-shy men.

And the more severely love-shy a man is, the earlier in life he is likely to have become deeply interested in the opposite sex from a romantic and esthetic standpoint. For example, almost 85 percent of the love-shy men who were studied for this book indicated that prior to the age of 13, they had been lonely for a close female companion. In contrast, none of the 200 self-confident men had felt the need. None of the non-shy had spent a lot of time daydreaming about girls when they were 10 or 11, whereas three out of every five of the love-shy men had.

The average love-shy man had his first romantic interest in the first grade when he was six, whereas the self-confident men were 11 years old and in grade six. Most middle-class children became romantically interested in the fourth, fifth, or sixth grades. So the love-shy men typically experience many long years of intensely-felt deprivation regarding the opposite sex. To be sure, most American males suffer some inhibitions when they are first romantically interested in a girl. But research shows that most of them suffer periods of emotionally-painful distraction for just three or four weeks. For many boys these painful periods may last for a mere fortnight or less. An average boy may suffer through two or three of these periods between the time of his initial romantic infatuation in the sixth grade and marriage say at age 24. So by that time, he will have had to deal with perhaps a total of eight or nine weeks of what a chronically love-shy male experiences from the time he is seven until he is an old man.

In most cases, if a child actually initiates a friendship with the object of his dreams, his preoccupations rapidly diminish. And the stronger the friendship, the less preoccupied he will feel.

"Oh, Leave Him Alone; He's Still Got Plenty of Time!"

Left to fester, love-shyness can quickly and easily become a permanent way of life. Some of the angriest and most bitter comments expressed in the hundreds of interviews I conducted for this book pertained to well-intentioned but misguided parents and relatives who had reacted to a respondent's lack of female friends and dating experience with the statement: "Oh, don't worry! Leave him alone! He's still got plenty of time!"

Love-shy males do not want to be left alone, their problems ignored and misinterpreted. They would like to overcome their shyness. The following remarks from a 39-year-old love-shy man poignantly reflect the rage many love-shy feel towards their parents' noncaring attitudes.

> I can remember lots of times my mother would have her friends over and someone would bring up the fact that I hadn't started dating yet. I was always delighted and thought that someone might finally do something for me. But my delight always quickly faded to depression because there was always someone there who would say "oh, leave him alone; he's still got plenty of time." And my stupid parents would go along with that bullshit reasoning. I didn't want to

be left alone, and I would always fervently pray that someone would do something for me that would somehow get me introduced to somebody. But that never happened. Today my parents never invite their friends over when I'm around. But for a really long time all I ever heard was this bullshit that I should be left alone because I've got plenty of time!

The nervousness most love-shy men show toward arranged introductions is typically misconstrued as antithetical by those wanting to help. Most shy people do not object to tactfully-arranged introductions by caring parents, relatives, teachers and friends.

The Preadolescent Love Experience

Virtually all of the love-shy men I interviewed had very clear and detailed memories of their preadolescent infatuations. Better than two-thirds had experienced one intense infatuation after another throughout elementary school. These intense fantasies had consumed a very great deal of the love-shys' time and psychoemotional energy until age 33 or 34 when the amount and frequency tended to drop off. But even in their 40s the love-shys still experienced occasional strong infatuations.

Sixteen percent of the older love-shys and seven percent of the younger ones had experienced their first infatuations as soon as they started school. Most of the love-shys saw members of their own sex as foreign. As one love-shy man said, "I viewed boys as members of another species." And since the teachers tended to discourage the love-shys from playing with girls, most of the love-shys were branded as social isolates at the outset of their education. A 41-year-old looks back:

> I remember the kindergarten teacher used to get all upset with me because she wanted me to play with the scooters and cars and a lot of other junk that the boys were playing with. I remember I tried doing those things on several occasions. And the praise and encouragement I got from the teacher made me feel really good because I really liked the teacher. But I just didn't enjoy it. In fact, I found it

painfully boring. And all the while I would be looking over at the girls and at the things I really wanted to do.

So I guess I just decided very early that I would have to sacrifice my need to please the teacher for my need to feel comfortable and please myself and just be myself. And after about November of my kindergarten year I never played on the floor with the boys again. I worked with craft things. And I became really good at making things out of clay.

I don't remember exactly when I first began to take really strong notice of them. But there were these two twin sisters in my kindergarten class, Rita and Ruth. They were fraternal twins. They looked entirely different. And before Thanksgiving I found myself looking all the time over at Ruth who was the really pretty one. By Christmastime it got to be really intense. When I went to bed at night I would think so intensely about her before I fell asleep that I would feel really warm and wispy and goosebumpy all over. Parts of my body would go moist, and I would dream that she was sleeping there beside me. You have to understand that I was just five years old at this time. Most of the psychiatrists I've told this to think that I'm putting them on. But I can remember Ruth as clearly as I can remember the things I did at work today. After all these years I've never forgotten her.

By March and April of my kindergarten year my mother was finally beginning to suspect that something was amiss. She thought something was wrong with me because I would come home from school and just sit on the cold front stoop, which was made of slate. And I would daydream intensely about Ruth. My mother kept insisting that I tell her what was bothering me. But I didn't have the nerve to say anything. Lots of time she chased me from the slate stoop because she thought I might catch a cold. Whenever that happened I just took a long walk and dreamed about Ruth. Sometimes my mother would scream at me when I came back because I had been away too long. But none of that phased me. I just wished that I could spend forever with Ruth.

Then one day in April of my kindergarten year it all sort of came to a head. My mother was taking me downtown to go shopping. And I was sitting with my mother on the bus. Whenever I went anywhere by bus with my mother she would always give me the window seat and she would sit on the aisle seat. I don't know what the hell happened; but this one time I was sitting in the aisle seat and my mother was sitting in the window seat. All of a sudden Ruth and her sister Rita and their mother got on the bus; and they sat with their backs to the window in that seat that's just at the entrance to the bus across from the driver.

Well, I started to blush, and I smiled uncontrollably. And I just couldn't control myself. I wanted to act like I didn't see them. And I started looking towards my mother—out the window. And she noticed that I was blushing. I mean, tears were coming down my face I was blushing and smiling so intensely! Anyway, my mother insisted that I tell her why I was blushing. And I asked her what she meant. I didn't know what the word blushing meant. Well, it didn't take long for my mother to guess what was happening because I had been okay until those people, including Ruth, got on the bus.

My mother guessed that I liked one of the little girls who got on. And she kept poking me about it. And I kept my mouth clamped shut more tightly than I ever kept my mouth shut in my life. A few stops before we had to get off my mother got up and went over to Ruth's mother and started a conversation with her. My mother always had a great deal more nerve than I ever did. I mean she could start conversations with strangers like that. Anyway, she found out from the lady that Rita and Ruth were in my kindergarten class. And when we got off the bus she started teasing me about which one of the two girls I liked, which was ridiculous because Rita wasn't pretty at all.

Anyway, she starts telling me that I shouldn't like either one of them because they were Jewish and we were Catholic. I remember I didn't know what she meant by that. All I know was that when my kindergarten year was over Rita and Ruth moved away. And for a long time I was really depressed because I didn't have the nerve to ask anybody where they moved to.

Some of the love-shys, on the other hand, came closer to developing relationships with girls during their prepubescent years than they ever did later on. Unfortunately, insensitive adults often tried to break up such relationships. If adults had been more understanding, they might have seen that allowing early romantic relationships to flourish might have prevented severe love-shyness from developing.

The following remarks of a 43-year-old man recall how as a child he had transcended the point of pure infatuation. He had actually interacted with his girl friend. And if this interaction had continued over time there can be no question but that some social self-confidence would have been gained. Even if the relationship had eventually died a natural death, this social self-confidence would have served this love-shy man well in regard to the practical problem of meeting and initiating meaningful relationships with other females in life.

I was only in kindergarten when I first fell in love. There was a girl in my kindergarten class who I found myself dreaming about all the time. But throughout all my years of education the love that I remember best of all was the one that I had had when I was in the second grade. I guess I didn't notice her too much right away. But after a couple of months I began to notice more and more this girl whose name was Phyllis. There were about 30 kids in my second grade class, about half girls and half boys. And whenever anything came up I always wanted to be either in or near the group that contained Phyllis. I started dreaming about her all the time. And nine times out of ten if the teacher called on me and I was off in a world of beautiful daydreams, it was Phyllis that I was dreaming about.

Well, one day when I was fooling around at home I saw my mother looking in some big book she had on the kitchen table. That was when I was introduced to the telephone directory. And I looked up the name "Springman," which was Phyllis' last name; and I found it there. And it also gave me her address.

Well, I already had a detailed street map of the town where I lived. I don't know why, but maps always fascinated me a very great deal. Even when I was only in the second grade I started to build up a tremendous collection of maps. I had them from every state in the union, and I had detailed street maps from all over. Anyway, I saw that Phyllis lived about a mile and a half away. But I had always loved to take long walks anyway. And I had a dog at that time which my parents always wanted me to walk.

So almost every day I would walk the mile and a half over to Woodside Drive. And I would walk up and down it several times with my dog. And each time I would approach that street, my fantasy life would become extremely rich. However, if I saw someone stirring in the window or on the front porch of the house where she lived, I would immediately become overcome by extremely strong anxiety feelings. And I would run like hell in the opposite direction for a few minutes. And then I would return. By the way, all of this happened in the spring of 1948. In 1956, when *My Fair Lady* opened, I immediately thought of Phyllis the first time I heard the song "On the Street Where You Live". And even today whenever I hear that song I always think of the street where she used to live where I would walk up and down with my dog Punch.

Well, about this time like when I would be staring at her in class she would begin smiling at me. I would start to blush. And I think the teacher became somewhat disturbed about this. Like the kindergarten and first grade teachers that I had had, this teacher was sort of perturbed about the fact that I never wanted to play with the boys. Anyway, after a few weeks I stopped blushing when our eyes met. I would smile at her and she would smile at me. But we still hadn't arrived at the point where we were actually saying anything to each other. But she knew I liked her. And I was very happy about the fact that she seemed to like that fact that I liked her. In fact, I don't think I've ever been so happy in my life, even though I was still too shy to start a conversation with her.

Well, one day when I was walking down her street with my wire-haired fox terrier her mom came outside and called me by name. At first I was extremely nervous and started to walk the other way. But she seemed very friendly, and she called me by name. She told me not to be afraid, and that she wanted me to come in and have some cream soda and cookies. Well, I felt extremely shy. But something made me turn around and start walking her way towards the house. Her mom seemed extremely nice, and when I walked in the kitchen Phyllis was there and she smiled and said "hi". And I finally became involved in my first real conversation with a girl!

That was in March of my second grade year. And from that point on we became very close friends. Every day as soon as school was over I would walk down to her house, and we would play together until dinner time. And then I would go home. My mother found out about my friendship with Phyllis. And she was glad I finally had somebody to play with even if it was a girl. One day my mother asked me to invite Phyllis home for lunch, and I did. And I remember we had lamb chops. And my mother seemed delighted with her. I was very happy. You have to understand, we didn't always agree about everything. I mean there were things I wanted to do that she didn't want to do. But it didn't matter. For about three months we were inseparable.

By the way, wouldn't it be great if even by the time you got to be of college age all you had to do was walk up and down a girl's street a few hundred times with your dog and you'd get invited in by her mother? That's one reason why I'd like to see arranged marriages become available in the United States, at least for shy people.

I remember I became eight years old pretty close to the end of the school year. And my mom threw a birthday party for me. Actually this was quite unusual because she only threw two parties for me while I was growing up; one in the second grade and one in the fifth. This particular party was a really special time for me because it was one of the very few times while I was growing up that I was really happy. My mom invited a lot of kids, some of whom had been teasing me quite a lot about spending all of my time with Phyllis. But I didn't care. I was glad to have them at my party. And strangely enough, I felt kind of pleased about things even though they were teasing me. Even though I had just turned only eight, I sort of suspected that some of the kids who were teasing me might have been jealous of me.

Shortly after that time my school let out for the summer. And my parents forced me to go away to summer camp. I always hated camp, but my dad always insisted that I go because he thought it might make me turn magically into his idea of a real boy. As you can see, that never happened. But what did happen was that when I arrived home at the end of the summer I didn't have the nerve anymore to go visit Phyllis. I had been looking forward to seeing her all summer long. But when I arrived home for some reason I somehow lost my nerve. Nevertheless, one day around Labor Day I did say that I was going to take a walk down there with my dog. And my mother told me she did not want me to go. She told me that she had this outing planned that would involve a lot of boys my age and their parents. And she insisted that I get ready to go on that. She was still after me to become a real boy.

I guess the real clincher, though, was the school. Both Phyllis and I continued attending the same school throughout our third, fourth, fifth and sixth grades. And I don't think it could have been purely chance by the wildest stretch of the imagination that we were kept separate for all four of those years. And you know even to this day I still feel very angry about that. Like if we had been together again in the third grade it would have been very easy for me to continue seeing her. Even if we had been separated for the third grade and put back together again in the fourth grade it would have been easy for me to start seeing her again. But the way they worked it, I just lost all the confidence that I had built up the preceding spring. One day when I was in the thrid grade I heard through the grapevine that both Phyllis and her mother were wondering why I didn't come around anymore. When I heard about that I felt really depressed. But I just didn't know what to do because by that time I had lost my nerve. And I was afraid that if I did try to see her again I wouldn't be able to think of enough things to say to her. And silence has always made me extremely nervous.

This boy's story poignantly illustrates how parents and other well-meaning adults often do far more harm than good in their dealings with love-shy and pre-love-shy boys. If the relationship had not been discouraged, this 43-year-old man might have developed social self-confidence and gone on to date and marry.

Beautiful, Driving Obsessions

There is a long-standing tradition in American society to belittle preadolescent infatuations. We use the term "puppy love" to make light of young love. Yet research strongly suggests that even very young children experience the emotions of love every bit as strongly as do those who fall in love at 18 or at 28 or 38. The past few years have yielded a great deal of new knowledge about the biochemical and neurological basis of love. The need for romantic love evidently manifests itself in many young children long before there is any capability of sexual performance. Many scientists now suspect that the need for heterosexual love and romance has a genetic basis that is distinct from the biological need for sexual expression. When one person perceives another as romantically appealing, a portion of the hypothalamus in the lower brain transmits a message by way of various chemicals to the pituitary. And in turn the pituitary releases hormones which rapidly suffuse the bloodstream, creating a more rapid heartbeat and a feeling of lightness in the head even in preadolescents. Simultaneously nerve pathways in and around the hypothalamus produce chemicals that induce—provided these chemicals are produced over a long enough period of time—what people refer to as "falling in love".

Love-shy men may have a hyperactive hypothalamus that responds to "love chemicals" significantly earlier in life than do most human beings. As I pointed out in Chapter Two, many components of the lower brain stem are much more hyper-reactive in introverts than in others. The "love nucleus" component of the hypothalamus is probably hyper-reactive in highly inhibited, very shy men as well.

In 1983, psychiatrist/neurologist Michael R. Liebowitz published a book called *The Chemistry of Love*, clearly documenting the point that the biochemical base for the emotion of love is the pituitary gland, whereas the biochemical base for sexual feelings and cravings lies in the gonads. Thus, in males testosterones released by the gonads create sexual feelings and cravings. In both sexes, the hormone phenylethylamine, produced and released by the pituitary, on the other hand, constitutes the biochemical basis for our "falling in love" response.

This finding finally provides us with a viable explanation for why some elementary-school youngsters fall deeply in love, very often years before they reach their adolescence. As I showed in Chapter Two, love-shy men tend to have a hyperactive HPA Stress Circuit. "P" for pituitary lies at the very heart of the HPA Stress Circuit. If a person's HPA Stress Circuit is normally revved up, we might reasonably assume that stepped-up electrical impulses in the pituitary overproduce phenylethylamine.

Phenylethylamine is a natural, endogenous chemical compound that impacts human beings in very much the same way as the amphetamine drugs. It is thought to affect the nervous system indirectly by inducing the brain to release large amounts of the neurotransmitters dopamine and norepinephrine, brain chemicals that tend to be high in inhibited people anyway.

Liebowitz's research strongly suggests that the neurochemical pathways serve to activate the response we call romantic attraction. Thus, the action of dopamine and norepinephrine appear to have a strong influence on the threshold, or activation level of the brain's pleasure center. Love (infatuation) brings on a giddy response that is very much like an amphetamine high. Thus, the crash that follows the breakup (or infatuation that doesn't go anywhere) resembles an amphetamine withdrawal.

Natural brain endorphins may also be involved in these feelings. When first discovered in brain and other body tissue, endorphins were called "the body's own morphine," because of their capacity to dull pain and produce euphoria.

Studying patients with a history of roller-coaster love affairs and/or of infatuations that just don't go anywhere, Liebowitz found that the affected individuals often had a craving for chocolate after a breakup or major disappointment in love. Chocolate has a high supply of the mood-altering chemical phenylethylamine. The brain may pour out its own chemical correlate to amphetamine (phenylethylamine) when a person is in love or infatuated with someone. And the brain may halt production of this chemical after a breakup or after a failed infatuation, thus leaving the person to suffer from its absence. Chocolate binges may simply be an attempt at self-medication, a way of easing withdrawal symptoms.

The research of psychologist John Money at Johns Hopkins University also suggests that love/infatuation has a distinctive physiological basis that is quite different from the physiological basis of sexual feelings and interests. Money found that persons who undergo surgery either before or during their teens for the removal of pituitary tumors almost always confront lifelong difficulty in falling in love. Although such individuals have been found to be fully capable of sexual arousal and intercourse, of expressing a wide range of human emotions, they do not seem to be able to experience full-blown love affairs.

All of these data suggest that there may be a physiologically-based reason as to why behaviorally inhibited, love-shy men tend to become deeply infatuated more frequently and earlier in life than more outgoing men.

Some social scientists have speculated that prepubescent love interest may be a reflection of a dearth of parental love. But normal boy-girl romance in elementary school does not appear to reflect any shortfall of family love. Professor Broderick's research showed that 57 percent of all children with unusually early heterosexual romantic interests enjoyed happy, loving relationships with their parents. The analogous figure for children who did not manifest such unusually early boy-girl romantic interests was 83 percent. Thus, in America there is only a mild association between early romantic interests and poor relationships with mothers and fathers.

In addition, these "early starters" were also more popular with same-sexed peers than were other children. Moreover, there are several hundred societies in the preindustrial world where children normally become interested in the opposite sex by the age of six or seven.

As I documented in Chapter One, people perform better, often much better, than they ordinarily do when they are involved in a reciprocal love relationship. This is especially true for males. But unrequited love taxes people's time and psychoemotional energies, causing destructive, self-defeating behavior.

The love-shy seven-year-old needs to be dealt with in the same manner as the love-shy 17- or 28-year-old. They all need to be helped to stop daydreaming and to begin to live by reaching out to the member of the opposite sex in whom they are interested. The fact that a majority of a love-shy child's classmates may not yet have romantic interests is immaterial. Preconceived timetables that everyone is supposed to fit need to be discarded.

Nearly all the love-shys spoke of resenting the unjust American custom of segregating the sexes. Many elementary and junior high-school social groups are gender-segregated, including Cub Scouts, Boy Scouts, Boy's Club of America, Campfire Girls, Brownies, Girl Scouts, YWCA and YMCA. Even at the senior high school level virtually all extracurricular activities continue to be gender-segregated.

A 22-year-old explains:

> I remember when I was about nine my dad made me join the Cub Scouts. It wasn't too bad; but I can remember dreaming all the time about girls being there instead of boys. I mean I took part in most of the activities, but I did so without saying much to anybody. Like, the kids used to refer to me as the "man of few words". I never really made many friends in the Cub Scouts even though I was with them for three years—all the way through the fourth, fifth and sixth grades.
>
> Maybe I can explain a little better what I mean. Like when I was about 11 we went on this overnight hike up around the Delaware Water Gap. And I enjoyed getting out into nature. But I didn't want to talk to anybody. All the guys found me unsociable, and the three fathers who led us on this trip I don't think liked me too much either. Like, I'd be off in a world of deep fantasy as I was walking

along. And I just didn't want to be interrupted from what I was daydreaming about because it was always much more beautiful than the stupid boring things the other 11- and 12-year-old boys were talking about—and the stupid, ridiculous songs they were singing!

Well, at that time I was really in love with the eight-year-old sister of one of the boys in my Cub Scout den. And I remember as I was walking along I would be dreaming that she was right there with me and that she and I were talking. And there would be other pretty girls in my classes who I would be daydreaming about. I mean, I'd see all of them there with me in my mind's eye. But most of the time I would be daydreaming just about my favorite girl—Jenny. She was my den mate's sister I just told you about. And even though I was just 11, I can remember getting moist and goosebumpy all over as I dreamed she was there inside my sleeping bag with me.

Anyway, when I was 12, I finally got out of the scouts, even though my parents didn't want me to. I just didn't see any point in staying in because I wasn't getting introduced to any girls. I mean, if my den group had been coeducational, there's no way in the world anyone could have ever gotten me to drop out. I just didn't want to participate in anything anymore where girls weren't present.

The love-shy men I studied knew better than their parents or teachers that they needed opportunities for relaxed, informal heterosexual interaction. Since this was denied them, they tended to withdraw from social activities organized for children and young people. The love-shy may well be "premature" in their strong desire for female companionship; but blocking the actualization of these fantasies may have led the boys to associate feelings of naughtiness and anxiety with the thought of being with a girl. In other words, the feeling that their desires for close, female companionship were somehow not right at that age may have grown into a more general anxiety about heterosexual companionship that remained with them long after they had arrived at an age when heterosexual interaction is considered appropriate by society. Unless a child is involved in a clearly dangerous activity, it is always best to both permit and encourage him to grow and develop in his own way.

Love in the Middle Childhood Years

Even though it is somewhat unusual for children to fall in love with opposite sexed age-mates as early as kindergarten or the first grade, by the fourth, fifth, and sixth grades such strong romantic attachments are quite commonplace throughout middle-class America. Love-shy boys differ in their romantic attachments from boys of normal psychoemotional adjustment in essentially seven ways. First (1) they become romantically interested in girls at least three or four years earlier, usually by kindergarten, the first or second grades; secondly (2), they rarely socialize with the object of their affections. (3) They are usually social isolates. (4) Their need to daydream about the object of their infatuation dominates the love-shys' lives so that they care very little about male peers, parents, schoolwork, little else, in fact. (5) Love-shy boys who don't like their own gender much prefer and need a coeducational environment for all activities. (6) The love-shy preadolescent tends to be strongly infatuated with just one girl at a time whereas his male peers tend to develop romantic interests in a lot of differenet girls. (7) The love-shy occasionally become deeply infatuated with television and movie actresses of their own age or younger whereas other boys confine their romantic interests to accessible girls.

The following interview with a 35-year-old love-shy illustrates typical behavior for a fifth grade love-shy boy. The love-shy boy daydreams while the adjusted, happy boy interacts. In this sense the two different lifetime scripts for the (love-shy and normal) boys begin to manifest themselves at about fifth grade. The adult social behavior of a love-shy man is little different from the behavioral style of the love-shy fifth grader.

> I didn't really do much after school until I got to be in the fifth grade. Up until that time I just sort of hung around. But that year they cleared a bunch of vacant lots about a half-mile from where I lived. And they created a park where kids could play at all kinds of stuff. I rode my bike there one day and I saw this really pretty girl. I didn't know her name, but I knew she was one grade behind me in school. All I can tell you is that love just all of a sudden hit me and I was overwhelmed. For the next two years I don't think I ever missed a single day at that park. I would take my bike there every single day after school. Most days she never came. In fact, I guess she only showed up there about once every two weeks or so. But that was enough to force me to go there every single day. I mean, if something held me up from getting to the park it was like I would be just

overwhelmed. My spirit would just be jumping out of my insides! Strange and really strong feelings would penetrate throughout my whole body. And I just couldn't stand still. I just had to get there even though I knew she might not show up.

Actually I never talked to her. All I ever did was look her way as long as she was anywhere near me. If she would look in my direction I would just feel overwhelmed as though hot lead had just passed throughout my entire bloodstream. And I would look away from her for a second. And then I would just run two or three laps around the park, or I might get on one of the swings and swing myself real hard. I think the other kids must have thought that I was crazy because sometimes I would just run and run whenever she would look at me. And as I would run or swing myself I would be dreaming about being in bed with her, or at the beach in the sun together, or just sitting quietly watching television together. This was long before I knew anything at all about sex.

After a while I guess she must have begun to suspect that I really liked her. But she never tried to start a conversation with me or anything. I never had the nerve to say anything to my mother or father about it. In fact, I never had the nerve to say anything to my folks about any of the girls I ever fell in love with. I just quietly suffered by myself all through my life.

Self-Disclosure Inhibitions

A particularly difficult problem is to get love-shy children to open up about problems, needs and desires. Before they will talk, they need plenty of warm, non-threatening encouragement. They must be able to trust the person to whom they confide and feel free to get in touch again whenever they need help.

Many school districts retain just one or two clinical psychologists, who are expected to trouble-shoot all the emotionally-disturbed youngsters. Obviously this is difficult to do with limited resources. A 37-year-old love-shy man shared this poignant story with me about how he had been too shy to tell a school psychologist what he really wanted to tell her during his one visit with her.

I remember I was in the third grade, and one day I was sent in to see the school psychologist because I was regarded as different than the other kids. They seemed to think that I needed help. Anyway, there were ten different elementary schools in our district, and this psychologist only came by our school about once every two weeks or so.

Well, I was given the entire school day with this psychologist. I was only about eight years old at the time, and it was really interesting. I mean she gave me all these tests. Most of the tests were spoken, so I didn't have to write anything. And she seemed to be a very nice person. Well, at one point she asked me to make a list of the three things I most wanted in all the world. I vividly remember this because she also said that I was definitely going to receive my number-one wish. I was just a little kid, and I remember her calmly saying that I'd better choose my number-one wish with care because I was going to receive it—whatever it was. She said that she had helped all the kids she had seen get the thing that they had listed as number one.

Well, I remember this more vividly than most other things in my childhood because the only thing I could think of was a girl friend. I knew I wanted a girl friend more strongly than anything else in the world. But I just didn't have the nerve to tell her that! There was this one girl in the other third grade class. Actually, she had been in my second grade classroom the year before. But now we had different third grade teachers. And what I really wanted was anything that might enable me to spend all my free time with her and make her my best friend.

Well, I remember I was stone silent for what must have been five minutes. It seemed like ages. And she was really confused about it. I mean I had done a lot of talking up to that point. And I took all her oral intelligence tests without any problems like this developing. She was really confused.

Well, what finally happened was that I said I'd tell her my second and third wishes first, and that I'd have to come back to wish number one. Well, I covered wishes number two and three rather fast. And then I began stalling again. This time instead of not saying anything I started elaborating on as many details as I could think of about my second and third wish. The funny thing is I couldn't tell you now what my second and third wishes were, even if my life depended on it. All I can remember is that I did a lot of talking about my second and third wish so that I would not have to talk about my first wish. I was really nervous and I wanted to bide myself some time. But I really couldn't think very easily because I was talking about something entirely different from what I was trying to think about.

Well, finally I just couldn't think of anything else to say. I couldn't stall her anymore, and I had to get to the first wish. Well, dammit, I just didn't have the nerve to tell her. So I finally told her that I wanted a dog! Actually I did want a dog, but that wasn't what I really and truly wanted more than anything else in the world. I wanted a girl friend, and I remember that for the rest of the school year I went through mental turmoil inside because I didn't have the nerve to tell her what I really wanted.

You know what? Well, I don't think two weeks went by before my father came home one night with a standard poodle puppy! I know neither of my parents had especially wanted a dog. I think this school psychologist must have talked to them. Anyway, this psychologist's prophecy was fulfilled at my expense! I was delighted to have the dog, but I would have exchanged it in an instant for what I really wanted. I didn't get my real number one. To this day I keep wondering what would have happened if I had told her what my real number one desire was!

To this 37-year-old man, the incident has taken on a kind of occult, mystical significance. However, even if the psychologist had been unable to grant him the specific girl he craved, she would have known what was on his mind. Without this information, she really couldn't help him. She couldn't find the root of his problem—the reason his third grade teacher sent him to see a school psychologist in the first place.

In this and similar cases, the child needs regular access to a trained psychologist, who knows various ways of eliciting information if the boy is too shy to express what's really on his mind. In the above instance, the child was ready to explain his true feelings and wishes when he received the dog. In fact, he may even have been ready to talk on the next school day—if he had been able to see the psychologist.

Media-Inspired Love Infatuations

Almost all the love-shy men experienced at least two romantic infatuations with media starlets before they reached college age. This is so even though most of the romantic infatuations that the love-shys had suffered through had involved accessible girls.

Several of the strongest and most intense infatuations mentioned by those interviewed had involved preadolescent girls. For example, one man told me that as a 14-year-old eighth-grader he had fallen in love with Brigette Fossey, the seven-year-old starlet of the French movie *Forbidden Games*. In fact, he had been so turned on by her and the movie that he sat through it 44 times. Another man had been so enthralled by film star Glynnis O'Connor that he sat through *Jeremy*, a film about teen shyness vis-a-vis the opposite sex, 86 times. And several people mentioned having sat through *David and Lisa*, and *Butterflies are Free* 40 or more times.

One of the most interesting comments came from a 44-year-old love-shy man concerning the family drama *I Remember Mama*, which ran on CBS Television every Friday night from 1949 until 1955.

Well, I guess there was only one television actress that I ever really fell in love with; and that was Robin Morgan. She played Dagmar on a program called *I Remember Mama*, which I used to watch all the time when I was a kid. Actually, I never really watched that much television compared to the amount that the other kids seemed to watch. But this was a program that I wouldn't miss for anything. And I remember it was on at a time which sometimes got me into trouble. Like, I was in junior high school for a lot of the time that it was on the air. And the school periodically threw parties. And the parties were always held on Friday nights. I can remember there were several times when I wanted to attend some social function at my school. But it was held on a Friday night. And I just couldn't go because if I did I would have missed Robin.

I remember some of the teachers used to accuse me of being antisocial. Actually this happened quite a bit because I remember I didn't have the nerve to tell them the real reason why I couldn't come. I remember they'd angrily come up to me and insist that I tell them what was so important that I couldn't come to the party. And I'd say something like "I don't know". My parents often got pissed off at me too. But I never had the nerve to tell them anything. They never would have understood.

Like if they only had held the parties on Saturday nights or even on Sunday nights. I know I would have gone to them. But I know I would have suffered immeasurably if I ever missed one of the *I*

Remember Mama programs. Like even if they had had video tape machines then as they do today I could have had the program copied while I attended the party. I even suggested to some of the teachers that if they started the functions at 8:45 instead of 7:30 I'd be able to come. See, *I Remember Mama* was only on from 8 to 8:30; and I could have gone anywhere after that."

Though this school was sophisticated enough to run social functions for its students, no staff was sensitive enough to pick up on what was actually going on in the boy's life. Without that, there was no way of helping him toward a viable solution to his love-shyness problems—having him meet some accessible girls.

Chapter 10

Sex and the Love-Shy

While all of the love-shys I studied were virginal, they did have sexual outlets.

Masturbation

Eighty-five percent of the older love-shys indicated that they averaged two or more ejaculations per week via masturbation, with a total of 4.18 ejaculations per week experienced through various modes of sexual self-stimulation.

In spite of being younger, 67 percent of the university aged love-shys averaged two or more ejaculations per week via masturbation and a total of 3.19 ejaculations per week.

In contrast, none of the non-shys averaged two or more ejaculations per week via masturbation. In fact, almost three-fifths of the non-shys told me that they never masturbated at all. Virtually all of the love-shy men masturbate. Parenthetically, the mean number of ejaculations averaged per week via masturbation by the non-shys was only 0.35—or about once each three weeks.

Of course, the self-confident non-shys were quite sexually

115

active with women. The non-shys had sexual intercourse on average 3.5 times per week. This may seem like a lot. But the significant comparison between the love-shys and the non-shys is their total weekly average. The older love-shys come up with a higher overall average of ejaculations than the 200 self-confident 19-24-year-old men. On a subjective level, all these love-shy men had been deeply involved in romantic fantasies involving highly-attractive women.

At 3.19 ejaculations per week, the younger love-shys were evidently the least sexually active of the three groups. And yet even this 3.19 figure can be considered somewhat high by comparison with what usually prevails for the typical sexually-active college student. For example, college men average with their lovers only 2.5 copulations per week. Allowing for additional masturbatory activity, it seems improbable that their total weekly average would be a very great deal higher than the 3.19 ejaculations per week average of the younger love-shy virgins.

Love-Shyness and Sexual Desire

The high incidence of masturbatory activity among the love-shys clearly suggests they are highly sexual people. But an exclusive reliance on frequent sexual self-stimulation does not provide a very satisfying sexual or emotional life. None of the love-shys seemed to feel any guilt about their masturbatory activities, but all felt severely frustrated by the fact that they were not living up to their true potential. Without women, they were all unhappy and dissatisfied.

Quite interestingly, masturbation reflects different emotional adjustment and mental health for college-aged females and males. For example, young men who masturbate three or more times per week tend to be unhappy, withdrawn, nonsociable, shy and rather poorly adjusted. On the other hand, among college-age females, such behavior has been found to reflect mental health, non-shyness, assertiveness, high levels of sociability, and social spontaneity, self-confidence, and happiness.

Felt Deprivation Creates Preoccupation

When a person is deprived for a long time of something he dearly wants, that person is highly likely to become intensely preoccupied and even obsessed with it. That may partially explain the unusually high frequency of masturbation among the love-shys. Love-shy men tend to be extremely interested in sex. They collect books on the subject and have copies of *Playboy* and *Penthouse* magazines strewn all over their apartments. And many of them have color photographs of attractive women, both nude and clothed, hanging on their walls. I did not observe anywhere nearly as much of this in the living quarters of the non-shy men.

In essence, sexual preoccupation is reflected in frequency of masturbatory activity. And it is certainly very often reflected in the frequent need to read about sex or to gaze upon the pictures of attractive women. In contrast, those whose sexual appetites are fairly well satisfied tend to have little need to read about the subject or to admire the photographs of inaccessible women. Perhaps more importantly, socially self-confident men are far less likely than severely love-shy men to be distracted by thoughts about sex. Thus, they are better able to concentrate on their work or on their academic responsibilities.

The Closet Heterosexual

The term "closet homosexual" describes the gay man or woman who has not yet "come out." The concept is also useful as a diagnostic label for the heterosexual man who does not date or interact with women even though he would much prefer to.

Whereas closet heterosexuality appears to be almost exclusively caused by severe love-shyness, closet homosexuality is attributable to the fear of being detected by potentially hostile employers, family, friends, and now the fear of AIDS. Because of the many constructive social and political changes brought about in the last two decades, closet homosexuality is a great deal less commonplace today than it used to be. Today most homosexuals eventually do come out of the closet, gaining enormously in mental health, personal pride and self-esteem. The only sort of "closet heterosexual" who is not love-shy is the Roman Catholic priest or other religious celibate. Recent studies have suggested that as many as 40 percent of these men are actually homosexual.

Male university graduate students without wives or girlfriends have much in common psychologically with men studying to become Roman Catholic priests. Using the *Minnesota Multiphasic Personality Inventory (MMPI)*, several researchers have found that both groups show below-average mental and emotional health. In fact, psychology graduate students and seminary students have MMPI profiles similar to long-term residents in mental hospitals. For example, both groups tend to score far above average on schizoid tendencies, a diagnostic category having to do with social withdrawal and social isolation.

Research has shown that students with close relationships with women earn significantly better grades than do those without. Moreover, after these men complete their studies, they move ahead in their respective fields significantly faster than do those who had avoided female companionship while in school.

The "Male Lesbian" Concept

Another potentially useful diagnostic label is that of "male lesbian." On the surface the whole idea appears ludicrous. Yet in selecting the men to be interviewed for this book the seemingly incongruous notion of "male lesbian" kept returning. For this reason, I don't think that any book pretending to be complete on the subject of chronic love-shyness in men can afford to ignore the "male lesbian" idea.

A "male lesbian" is a heterosexual man who wishes he had been born a lesbian woman. Unlike the transsexual, the "male lesbian" does not feel he is a woman trapped inside a man's body. None of the love-shy men entertained fantasies about sex-change operations. All wanted to keep their male genitalia; all wanted to remain as males. But all envied the prerogatives of the female sex, believing that these prerogatives better fitted their own inborn temperaments. The following represents a typical comment from a love-shy man:

> From the time I was very, very young, I had always wished that I had been born a girl. I know I would have been much happier as a girl

because I have always been attracted to the kinds of things that girls do. But every time I think about how great it would have been if I had been born a girl, I immediately realize that if I had been born a girl I would be a lesbian. I have always strongly disliked the idea of doing anything with my own sex. I despise men. Just thinking about making love to a man, even as a woman, makes me want to throw up! But I would also never want to play football or baseball or any of the other games boys are supposed to like playing. I never wanted to have *anything* to do with the male sex, on any level. So, like if I had been born a girl as I would have wanted, I would definitely be a lesbian because I'd be falling in love with and having sex with girls instead of with men. (40-year old heterosexual love-shy man.)

"Male lesbians" differ from transsexuals and homosexuals in that they cannot conceive of making love to a man. Thus, after sex change surgery the male transsexual almost always wants to begin making love *to a man* AS A WOMAN. The male homosexual wants to make love AS A MAN *to a man*. On the other hand, the "male lesbian" wishes that he had been born a woman. But he always makes it clear that if he had indeed been born a woman he would be a full-fledged lesbian. In other words, he would want to socialize exclusively with women and would choose female partners exclusively for love-making. In short, a secret fantasy of many love-shy men is to be a beautiful woman who lives with, and makes love to, another beautiful woman.

The love-shy men all reluctantly accepted the fact that they are males. And none had ever experienced any urge to dress up as a woman. Since they could not be women, most visualized themselves as men romancing beautiful women. And most of them had begun doing this from a much earlier age than the majority of non-shy heterosexual men. Thus, at age eight they would spend hours daydreaming about romancing a beautiful little girl.

In sum, the "male lesbian" (1) does not want to play with males, (2) does not want to make love to or experience sex with males, (3) does not have male recreational interests, and (4) does not even want to procreate male children. The vast majority of the love-shy men confessed that if they ever became a father they would want girl children only and NO BOYS. In contrast, only one percent of the self-confident, non-shy men felt that way. In fact, the non-shy men preferred the idea of fathering male children to the idea of fathering female children by a ratio of almost three to two.

Sexual Attitudes and Values

Is sexual prudery or moral conservatism related in any way to love-shyness or its development? Surprisingly, 91 percent of the older love-shys and 79 percent of the younger ones believed that monogamous, contraceptively protected premarital sex is socially acceptable. In fact, only six percent of the older love-shys and 11 percent of the younger ones would never want to experience premarital sex under any circumstances. Yet none of the love-shy men approved of casual or promiscuous premarital sex. Their attitude towards sex was decidedly romantic and one night stands were tabu. In contrast, 73 percent of the self-confident men accepted some casual or promiscuous premarital sex.

All three groups believe that premarital cohabitation is okay. Approximately 85 percent approved of monogamous premarital cohabitation as an integral part of courtship. And most would like to engage in it themselves. But the attitudes of the love-shys were substantially more romantic than those of the non-shy men. Whereas most of the non-shys indicated that they would be enthusiastic about cohabitating with any willing girl, the love-shy men would only want to live with someone they deeply love.

The great majority of shys and non-shys believe nude beaches should be available.

Hence, I drew a key conclusion from these data that there are very few if any significant differences between non-shy and love-shy men as far as attitudes toward human sexuality are concerned. Conservative or prudish sexual attitudes appear to have no bearing at all on why or how the love-shy got to be the way they are.

Being Misperceived as Homosexual

As extremely passive people, some of the love-shy men had experienced difficulties in fending off homosexual strangers they met on buses, subways or in other public places. Typically an aggressive homosexual would move his hand onto the love-shy man's crotch area. The love-shy man would then become extremely nervous and upset and change his seat or otherwise move away.

In at least one situation recounted by a 20-year-old love-shy man, getting away was not easy:

Well, this happened during the week between the end of the spring quarter and the beginning of the summer quarter. I didn't want to go home because I figured it just wouldn't be worth it for only one week. So I stayed in the dormitory. Anyway, one night I left the student union building after having some refreshments, and I started walking back to my dorm room. All of a sudden this guy comes up to me and starts acting really friendly. He said he had just come down here from Eugene, Oregon, and was lonely and wanted to meet some people. There was something about him I didn't like; but I couldn't put my finger on anything except his very hoarse, raspy voice. I had often been lonely myself; so I didn't want to seem unfriendly. Anyway, he invited himself into my dorm room, and everything was okay for the first fifteen minutes or so. But then he asks me to remove one of my shoes. I thought that was a strange request, but I did it for him. And he held the shoe up really close to his eyes. I thought he was trying to read something in it. Anyway, next he asks me to take my socks off; and then I knew something was fishy! All of a sudden he rushes down and takes my socks off. He holds them up to his nose real hard. And I was shocked. I didn't know what to say or do. Then he grabs my foot and holds that real hard up to his nose and puts it in his mouth! I start screaming; but I was really worried because I knew there weren't many people around who could hear me. This guy starts grabbing me and trying to force me on to my bed. I don't know how I did it, but I managed to grab for the door knob, and I managed to get it open. By that time the guy had ejaculated, and you could see all this stuff staining right through his pants. He had so much nerve! Believe me, that wasn't the end of him. He tried to get into my room on three more occasions before I finally saw the last of him. I mean he would stand outside my door sometimes for an hour at a time asking me to let him smell my feet. I couldn't even leave my room to take a leak because he'd be standing out there trying to get at my feet!

Almost all of the love-shy men claimed that they were often mistakenly perceived as homosexual. In fact, for many of the older love-shys this misconstrual was an almost daily occurrence. People who saw these love-shy men with any degree of regularity or frequency would begin to notice that they were never with anybody. As a result of never being seen in the company of a woman, acquaintances in their apartment building or dormitory would begin to suspect homosexuality. And some of these people would occasionally become quite overt in the manifestation of their suspicions.

Many of the love-shys could remember receiving a steady barrage of ego-disparaging name-calling (e.g., fag, queer, fairy, faggot, etc.) from the earliest grades of elementary school onward. Even when old enough to learn the meaning of these labels, they never believed themselves to be homosexual. The labels, they thought, merely reflected the gross stupidity and callous insensitivity characteristic of all bullies.

Many sociologists believe that long exposure to a particular disparaging label results in the internalization of that label and the transformation of the labeled person's self-image. According to this theory, a teenager who is frequently labeled a fag by many different people on a daily basis would in time actually become one. This labeling theory did not prove valid for any of the 300 heterosexual love-shys. The verbal abuse had acted instead to lower self-esteem.

During their childhood, physical bullying had bothered the love-shys a great deal more than verbal hazing. But as adults, most of the love-shys were very bothered by all the intimations behind their backs that they are homosexually inclined. The whisperings were proof that they were not in charge of their lives. The love-shys felt even worse off than most homosexuals. While there is a heavy price to be paid for being "gay," a homosexual can at least pay the price knowing he is true to himself. But the heterosexual love-shy man, especially after the age of 30, is often required to pay the price for being something he is not . . . unable to enjoy any of the rewards, support groups, and emotional security that come with being a homosexual.

Chapter 11

Obsessions, Compulsions, and Interpersonal Anxiety

Love-shy males tend to be very unhappy. It is the nature of unhappiness to make its victims behave in ways that cause others unhappiness, turmoil and tension. Strong believers in the morality of compassion and empathy, love-shy men tend to have humanitarian ideals. They almost never intend to hurt others or to create problems or anxieties for them. But because their own deepest needs are not met, they don't always behave well.

Staring and Following Behavior

Ninety-seven percent of the older love-shys and 71 percent of the young ones often stared at attractive girls, while only 11 percent of the self-confident men behaved in the same way. And 42 percent of the older love-shys and 31 percent of the younger ones had at one time or another gotten into trouble because of their inability to stop themselves from staring at girls they found very attractive. Only nine percent of the non-shys had ever gotten into any trouble for this sort of behavior. Contributing to the compulsive quality of this staring behavior and greatly enhancing the compulsion to stare, were hours spent fantasizing about these attractive women. But whenever an attractive woman looked as though she might make a move toward a love-shy man, he would become overwhelmed with fright and turn his head or walk away.

Needless to say, this sort of behavior was very unnerving to most of the women who had been victimized by it. And they did not know how to respond to it. Some who became quite worried or even frightened went to the police or the college dean or campus security to try to get something done about it.

When the love-shy man got into trouble, he was always very hurt because he typically fantasized that his love-object was a kind of goddess who would somehow understand him. One young man who had grown up in a small community in Alabama, spent a night in jail for following a girl around after receiving several warnings to stop. Several other love-shys suffered bruises and welts as a result of being accosted by male friends or brothers of attractive women. The most common punishments were university disciplinary action or job termination.

One 35-year-old love-shy man told how he was suspended from college:

> I grew up here in Los Angeles. But I wanted to attend the University of Montana because I wanted to see what life was like outside this city. I didn't get along very well with my folks. And I had heard that the people up in Montana were supposed to be much friendlier than those here in L.A. I mean, I really thought that if the people were really friendlier as everybody was saying, then I should be able to get some girl to come after me. You know what I mean? Like I figured that sooner or later some girl up there would make friends with me, and everything would be okay from that time onward. I could get married if I could get the right, friendly girl to make friends with me.
>
> Well, my father was a successful accountant, and he had enough money to pay the out-of-state tuition up there in Montana. And I was really looking forward to moving up there because, like, I went to high school in Canoga Park. And Valley girls are just all shit! I mean, they're just not romantic. I wanted to get a girl as fast as I could who would be really romantic and beautiful.

When I got up there I was really bitterly disappointed. I mean the countryside was nice enough. I used to enjoy taking long drives all over. But everybody ignored me. And even though my father was paying for a double room for me in the dormitory, by March of my freshman year I ended up having the room all to myself. And in my sophomore year my roommate moved out by Columbus Day weekend, and they didn't assign me anyone else. So I had my double room all to myself all during my sophomore year. And I used to dream a lot about how nice it would be if I could get a girl in there with me. I had the place all to myself, and it would have been so beautiful.

Anyway, it took until my sophomore year until I spotted someone who I really liked. This girl was a freshman, and she had the most beautiful long, dark hair you ever saw. She had a really beautiful face with a kind of ethereal look to it, like she had come from some other world. And she had blue eyes and narrow thin legs. I mean she was really perfect! But I had never dated anyone in my life, and I knew that I couldn't just go up to her and say anything.

So pretty soon I began making mental notes of the times of day and places around campus where I saw her. I spotted her a lot in the library; and I couldn't take my eyes off of her. I couldn't concentrate on a thing. I'd sometimes have my book turned to the same page for hours on end whenever she was there. And by Thanksgiving I was following her all over the campus. Several times she looked like she was going to approach me. And I got so frightened I had to go to the bathroom. I mean, I was just shaking all over. I knew I wanted her more badly than life itself. But I would shake all over whenever she would turn around and look my way.

Anyway, one day this big, tough-looking adult accosted me as I was peering through a first floor window at her where she was attending a math class. The guy showed me a police badge. And I was really shocked. I mean this guy looked like an overgrown, overaged football player. He wasn't wearing a uniform or anything. Anyway, he asked for my student 'ID', and took down all the information on it. And he said I'd soon be hearing from the dean.

Well, I got called into the dean's office the next morning. In fact, he made me cut my English class in order to come because he said it was extremely important. Anyway, after I got there he started asking me all these questions I was just too shy to answer. And then he said he was going to send me to the university psychiatrist; and that if I was caught anywhere near this girl again I would be suspended.

Well, my insides felt like they were being torn out. I mean I realized that there wasn't any way I could really ignore this girl. I had been spending 24 hours a day dreaming about her, and she was a part of me. There was no way I could just forget she existed. I mean, just one look at her made my day; although it also made my heart beat extremely hard, and it made me feel almost out of breath just to look at her.

I went to the shrink because I had to. And he was just as bad as the shrinks my father sent me to back home. In fact, I'd say he was even worse because he was extremely condescending towards me. And he said he couldn't do anything about getting me introduced to any girls. I mean if he wouldn't make any effort to introduce me to any girls, I figured he was worthless to me. I mean, what good is any psychiatrist unless they give you what you need? I needed a girl I could love. And whenever I asked him to introduce me to some girls all he ever did was ask me what my feelings were about his refusal to do so! Isn't that the stupidest damn thing you ever heard? Psychiatrists are all for the shits! I never met a one I really liked because they don't want to give you the kind of help you really need!

Anyway, to make a long story short, I was accosted again by this plainclothesman about a week before Christmas vacation was scheduled to begin. There was no way I could make like this girl didn't exist on the same campus with me. And the dean suspended me for it. I lost a whole year of work because of this incident. It was really the most painful time of my life because no one would give me the help I really needed. When I got home my parents were more hateful of me than ever. My father sent me to this expensive shrink in Santa Monica. And it was the same old shit. This time the psychiatrist was a nice guy. But just like all the others he wouldn't do anything to really help me except for one thing. He did put me into a group therapy situation where there were some girls. But most of them were too old for me. And the one girl there of my age was just too damned hostile.

Some love-shys got into trouble writing love-letters to girls they were infatuated with. For example, a love-shy man might find the girl's name and address in her books and papers while she was away from her library study table. After receiving love letters from these shy men, the women often became very nervous and upset. Often they would respond by going to the police or the dean, further disillusioning the love-shys.

One love-shy man had been fired and another called on the carpet at work because of love letters they had surreptitiously sneaked onto the desks or into the lockers of young women. In both cases, the young women took these innocent love letters to the boss. They didn't know these young men, and the letters made them nervous. But their punishing response proved traumatic to the love-shy men, who became more fearful of women than ever.

Of the men who got in trouble, 62 percent got into trouble a second time after staring at or following a different girl. And 38 percent were disciplined a third time.

Because it is easier to hide as well as to deny, the recidivism rate for staring at girls is much higher than it is for following them. One university man even brought a movie camera on campus and hid himself behind windows, shrubs and doorways where he filmed his loved one. Some of the older love-shy respondents admitted even now they occasionally find themselves repeatedly staring at someone they find attractive.

Applying Pressure Upon Parents

The intractable obsession that many love-shys had with respect to their need for intimate female companionship often prompted non-shy behavior toward their parents. Many of them tried to prod their parents into using their social connections to help them meet eligible young women. But none was successful. The following remarks from a 39-year-old man illustrate the difficult psycho-dynamics of intractable love-shyness.

> After I had completed three years of graduate school I decided to take off a year. I thought I'd go back to Denver where my parents still lived, and see if I could force them to get me a girl. My father was a successful lawyer, and I knew that he must have had all sorts of connections in the local community. So I thought maybe I could get him to get me a wife. I was just getting more and more depressed all the time. And even though my grades were good and I had success-fully completed a Masters degree, I knew that I would be much more effective if I had a wife. A lot of the students in my classes were

already married. And I was just desperate. I was willing to do just anything to force my parents into doing something for me to get me a wife.

Well, up to that time I never had the nerve to say anything to my parents about my shyness problems. They thought I was just a slow starter, and like my mother would always keep saying to her friends that I had plenty of time, and I'd get over my bashfulness when the right woman came after me. Well, no woman had ever come after me. And my father kept telling me that I was really lucky. At the dinner table ever since I was a small kid he would tell me "ahhh, never get married, kid!" He kept saying that even though he had been married to my mother for over 30 years without very much evident fighting or turmoil between them.

Well, I had just turned 25 when I left my graduate school in Seattle. My parents gave me a really cool reception. They couldn't understand why I had turned down my student stipend and would want to return to live with them. Both of them bitched away and bitched away at me to get a job and stop living at home with them. And I kept telling them that I'd leave as soon as they got me a 'goose'. I don't know why. But it was just much easier for me to use the word 'goose' with them. I didn't have the nerve to say 'girl'.

Anyway, they started getting madder than hell at me. Whenever they had company, which was quite often, I would tack or scotch tape little announcements to the wallpaper or to the guests' cars which said: "Please get my parents to get me a goose! Mention this to my parents and they'll explain it".

Then I started doing all kinds of other stuff. Like after my parents went to bed I would take all the cans of food out of the kitchen cabinets, and pile them up one on top of the other, until they went from the floor to the ceiling. And I would leave them balanced like that. My parents thought I was going nuts. And I just kept telling them that I wouldn't stop until they got me a goose. I mean I told them that they hadn't finished their responsibilities with me yet.

Even though I was 25, they still had to get me a goose; then they would be finished with their child-rearing responsibilities with me. Like, there are societies all over the world where the parents take upon themselves the responsibility of finding geese for their children. Well, I thought I could force my parents to get me a goose—I mean 'wife'.

Well, one time my father came home and told me that he might be able to get me a date with one of his secretaries. Actually I kind of liked the girl he had in mind. She was sort of pretty. But I had never met her. I mean, at a business meeting my father took me to he introduced me to her. But he didn't do anything to enable us to sit down and really get to know each other. I mean, I didn't have the nerve to say anything after I said 'hi'. She was busy mixing whiskey sours for all these businessmen. And I didn't have the nerve to go up and try to talk to her—although my father was creating something of a scene trying to force me. Like he just wasn't cool. If he could have only set something up where we would have to talk to each other without me feeling any anxiety, it would have been great.

Anyway, a few days later my father came home and told me that he had told this girl that she should be expecting a telephone call from me. And she had allegedly said 'great' to my father. So for the next several days my father was constantly at me to call. And believe me, I desperately wanted to call this girl because she did seem really nice. But I just couldn't bring myself to get up the nerve. I mean, what could I say? How would I even begin? I just couldn't handle the situation. And my father just became more and more pissed off at me. He kept telling me that I had embarrassed him at work because this girl had been expecting me to call; and I didn't call. I kept telling my father that she was a really nice goose, but that he'd have to work something out that would make it easier for me to get involved in a conversation with her. Anyway, he just got to the point where he just kept telling me to go to hell.

Well, I wouldn't stop with my parents because I had told my classmates back at the U. of Washington that I was taking off a year to find a wife, and that I'd be returning as soon as I had found one. Anyway, I started doing all kinds of crazy things like putting a wet mop on my mother's living room broadloom, and overflowing the toilet bowl. One time when my parents weren't home I took a lot of my mother's stuff down to the pawn shop. I didn't need the money and I wasn't stealing anything because I gave them the pawn tickets and loan money as soon as they got home. I just told them that I wouldn't stop doing these things until they finally fulfilled their responsibilities with me and got me a goose.

Well, my father had me arrested and I spent a night in jail. My father bailed me out the following morning even though he was the one who had me arrested. By this time I was just so frustrated and exasperated about my parents' unwillingness to do anything to help me that I decided to go back to graduate school. I mean even their friends didn't seem to notice all the pleas for help that I had left around in the form of these notes saying that I needed a goose.

Well, I finally went back to graduate school. But I had to go to Oregon instead of back to Washington—because I didn't have the nerve to face the kids and tell them that I hadn't made any progress at all in my quest for a wife.

On the surface these aggressive tendencies of this man appear antithetical to shyness. But they are actually loud pleas for help.

Grossly immature behavior and chronic misbehavior are ways of trying to get attention when normal modes of communication are ignored or fail to work.

Difficulties Concentrating

The obsessions of the love-shy burn a tremendous amount of psychic energy that could be used for constructive purposes. Obsessive and compulsive thoughts, most of which pertain to their deprivation of female companionship and love, prevent love-shys from concentrating their energies on constructive activities and endeavors. Eighty-four percent of the older love-shys and 62 percent of the younger ones had trouble concentrating in contrast to only six percent of the non-shys.

Occasionally some of the love-shys suffered from obsessive thoughts even when engaged in recreational activities. For example, one 50-year-old man comments:

> Sometimes like when I am at a movie I won't be able to concentrate because I'll have these thoughts that I just can't allow myself to forget. Sometimes these thoughts aren't even really important, although other times I'll want to remember them for some reason. So I always carry paper and pen with me no matter where I go. Like when I'm watching a movie I'll be able to concentrate on things better if I simply write down my thought—even if it's an unimportant thought. And so I write it down. And then the movie will remind me of some other idea. And again I won't be able to concentrate and enjoy the film until I write it down. I have over 3,000 note cards with these ideas on them. I keep them in a

disorganized mess, and I never look at them. But I just couldn't throw them out because at one time or another I just couldn't concentrate on something until I wrote down an idea on one of the cards.

A 24-year-old man said:

Sometimes something will happen that will make me forget what I was thinking of. I really hate more than anything to forget what I was thinking of. And sometimes I'm in mental turmoil for a long time whenever this happens, unless I can make the thought come back to me. Like if I forget a thought while I'm listening to a lecture or watching a movie, I just won't be able to concentrate for the rest of the presentation. I get so upset that I almost cry when this happens. That's why I become so upset if somebody knocks on my door, and the knocking causes me to forget what I had been thinking. That can really ruin my whole evening—unless I get lucky and I can remember what it was I had been thinking of.*

Sense of Humor

Given the anxiety problems, the people-phobia, and the obsessive thoughts, the love-shys sadly grew up to be adults with inadequate senses of humor.

Yet sense of humor is one of the ingredients that American women deem to be most important in a man. In fact, several studies show that a sense of humor is of formidable predictive value for a successful marriage. A relaxed sense of humor is a major element of communication skills.

The unhappiness of the love-shys' formative years makes them extremely self-centered, self-conscious and self-preoccupied, unable to laugh at themselves or life's discrepancies. Whereas fully 100 percent of the non-shy men laugh a lot, just 22 percent of the younger love-shys and a mere six percent of the older love-shys do.

---

*Obsessive-compulsive disorders have recently been linked to an excess of serotonin in the brain. Serotonin is one of the neurotransmitters of which very shy introverts have also been found to have too much. (See Chapter 2 of this book.)

On the other hand, 63 percent of the older love-shy men and 45 percent of the younger ones say they seldom laugh. Only 20 percent of the older love-shys and 34 percent of the younger ones find it easy to laugh. Several told me that as young children they laughed quite easily, but that they had somehow lost the ability over the years. In fact, one 39-year-old love-shy man told me that it has probably been approximately 20 years since he had laughed.

The ability to laugh is important not only for making a person attractive to others but for his own health. Several studies have shown that laughing aids digestion, circulation, blood pressure and enzyme activity. And laughter, of course, has a strong bearing on mental health.

All of the non-shy men said they get a lot of fun out of life, compared to only 23 percent of the older love-shys and 35 percent of the younger ones. In a related question, 95 percent of the non-shy men said that they were "very good at being happy" versus only four percent of the older love-shys and 11 percent of the university-aged love-shys.

American men are trained not to display feelings and emotions. The pathologically love-shy are especially vulnerable in this regard. For example, 93 percent of the older love-shys and 66 percent of the younger ones agreed that they found it very difficult to display emotion or feeling. Even among the non-shy men the analogous figure was a surprisingly high 19 percent.

Interpersonal Anxiety and Social Avoidance

A set of experiments conducted in 1959 by Stanley Schachter demonstrated that people confronting a stressful experience will tend to seek the informal social support of other people—even strangers if necessary. Some subjects were told they were going to experience a series of painful electric shocks while others anticipated only very mild electrical stimuli. The two groups were given a choice between waiting alone and waiting with other subjects for a brief time while preparations were made. Schachter found that the greater the anticipated pain, the greater the tendency for subjects to wait amid the companionship of other people. He interpreted this pattern as reflecting heightened need for reassurance, distraction, information and social comparison among subjects experiencing greater stress.

In 1961, Philip Zimbardo replicated Schachter's results. But he went further by demonstrating that people do not always seek social affiliation or emotional support in the face of severe stress or anticipated pain. Zimbardo distinguished between fear of an inherently dangerous object and anxiety stemming from an awkward social situation.

In Zimbardo's anxiety study, male college students anticipated having to suck on baby-bottle nipples and pacifiers. There was far greater variation in emotional arousal in the anxiety experiment than in the fear condition. Subjects experiencing anxiety had a marked preference for waiting alone. Almost all subjects experiencing fear chose to wait with other people.

Zimbardo suggested that if people are embarrassed they will tend to fear informal social contact. Even emotional support only serves to increase their anxiety. Because the anxious person is aware that his feelings are inappropriate, he is loath to communicate his anxieties to other people. To avoid being ridiculed or censured, he conceals anxiety which he suspects others in the same situation don't feel and which he believes ought not to upset him.

Deep down the love-shy man is clearly embarrassed about his inability to connect with any woman. Since women do not constitute an objectively dangerous sort of stimuli, the painful inability to approach and to initiate conversations with them represents an anxiety, not a fear. In American society, it is socially unacceptable for men to harbor anxieties. It is even more socially unacceptable for men to permit their lives to be virtually governed by their anxieties.

The lives of the love-shy are, in point of fact, quite governed by their anxieties. And I believe that this represents a formidable reason as to why virtually none of the 300 severely love-shy men had any strong desires to informally affilitate with other men. Many of the love-shy men specifically told me that once they managed to get themselves a girl they would definitely want to have some male friends. But until then—because of their socially unacceptable anxieties—they felt very uncomfortable with fellow males, whom they might otherwise have enjoyed as friends.

This is a key reason why I believe that love-shy males of all ages (including prepubescents) must first be therapeutically helped to informally affiliate with women/girls. I believe this must be done before they will be amenable to therapy aimed at the cultivation of same-sexed friendships. As long as love-shy males desperately crave female companionship, and as long as they are governed by these socially unacceptable anxieties which cause them to avoid opportunities for friendly intercourse with women, they will go to considerable lengths to avoid sociable interaction with fellow males.

Another experimental study with clear implications for our understanding of love-shy males was conducted in 1968 at Stanford University by Jonathan Freedman and Anthony Doob. Using a clever experimental maneuver, they made some of their subjects feel different from those around them, whereas other experimental subjects were made to feel pretty much like others of their own age and sex. Hence, subjects who were told (after taking a battery of personality tests) that they were very unlike others of their own age and sex tended to elect working alone on a contrived experimental task. This was especially true if none of the other experimental subjects in the room knew that they were actually deviant. The rest of the experimental subjects chose to work in a group with other people.

These nonconformist men tend to be embarrassed about their behavior, which is at variance with their own value systems. They are embarrassed about the way their anxiety about women has dominated their lives. Thus, we might reasonably guess that most of them don't especially care to be found out or exposed—as could quite easily happen within an all-male peer group.

People who feel "different" from others of their age and sex are highly unlikely to want to associate with friendship groups composed of same sexed peers. Their desire to hide their deviancy until it is rectified will make them prefer solitude to being in the company of others who might become hostile and disapproving.

Chapter 12

Medical Symptoms and Sensitivities

The human mind and body function as a holistic unit. The mind constantly affects the body in a variety of ways just as the body affects the mind. Thus, our lifestyles, reflecting relative degrees of inborn behavioral inhibition or extroversion, affect our bodies and minds.

It should hardly come as a surprise, then, that severely shy people have a vulnerability to certain kinds of medical symptoms while remaining less susceptible to others. I asked all 500 respondents a large number of questions about their health in general and about psychosomatic symptoms in particular.

Symptoms Not Related to Shyness

In the United States medical doctors receive more complaints about headaches than any other single symptom. And more over-the-counter remedies are sold for headaches than for any other kind of symptom. Yet only one-fifth of the severely shy and non-shy men said that they suffered from frequent headaches.

My findings were even more surprising in regard to back

trouble. Only one in 20 shy men were found to suffer from such problems compared to one in ten among the non-shys. Back trouble costs American business more money each year than any other type of medical problem apart from headaches and alcoholism. Perhaps the love-shy are less susceptible because they don't participate in athletics.

Very few love-shy or non-shy men suffer from constipation, diarrhea, "chronic gas," stomach aches, insomnia, cramps, or ulcers.

Cortisol and the Headcold Problem

On the other hand, my research data provided strong evidence that there are certain kinds of medical problems for which the behaviorally inhibited are far more susceptible than the majority of the population. Topping the list of complaints is the common headcold.

Many readers of this book will be familiar with "Adelade's Lament" from the musical comedy *Guys and Dolls* in which her almost constant headcold symptoms fluctuate in severity with the level of doubt that she feels about her boyfriend's love for her. But how do we explain the connection between shyness and headcolds? The earlier chapters of this book provide clues. Shy people (who tend to perceive and react to the world as a much more stressful place than socially self-confident people) tend to have more of the stress hormone cortisol in their bloodstreams. And cortisol tends to reduce the efficacy of the body's defense system by weakening enzymes that promote the killing of germs.

I did not, however, find the love-shys to be more susceptible than non-shys to the influenza virus, perhaps because they socialize less than the others.

Itchy Nose

Chronically shy people often suffer from attacks of itchy nose, and scratching an itchy nose with germ-infested fingers is another way of catching a cold.

Intense itching inside the nose may be caused to some extent by nasal polyps and deviated septum. Any obstruction making it difficult for mucous to pass will result in dried-up phlegm in the nasal cavity, causing a person to feel a need to pick his nose.

Allergies

Two-thirds of the love-shys had been diagnosed at some point in their lives as having one or more allergies versus none of the self-confident. Harvard psychologist Jerome Kagan has also found that severely shy children tend to suffer from chronic allergies. Kagan speculates that here again cortisol may come into play. As one of the effects of cortisol is to suppress the immune system, there is very likely a close connection between high reactivity to stress and a vulnerability to a wide variety of chronic allergies as well as to headcolds.

Frequently Blocked Nasal Passages

By far the great majority of love-shy men had difficulties breathing through the nose.

Implications for Shyness Prevention

Some people are born with a condition known as "deviated septum and polyps". Males and people of northern European ancestry are more vulnerable than others. The septum, the cartilage which separates the two nostrils, may be deviated so that one nostril is smaller than the other and mucous doesn't drain properly.

People with allergies appear to be susceptible to nasal polyps. The polyps, which develop in the upper respiratory tract as a way of preventing pollens from getting into the interior of the body, greatly impede nasal breathing.

Nasal polyps and deviated septum prevent the flow of mucous out of the body and often prevent air from coming in. When the victim catches cold, he is likely to suffer more than others. This is partly because the polyps provide germs with more places to hide.

While few of the men studied had consulted a rhinologist or nasal specialist, their symptoms sounded like deviated septum and nasal polyps.

My first recommendation to any love-shy person with chronic nasal breathing problems is to seek a rhinologist. A person with nasal breathing difficulties may not get enough oxygen to the brain, especially during sleep. Love-shy men have considerable difficulty thinking quickly and clearly under stress. A person who breathes freely through the nose may be getting significantly greater amounts of oxygen than the person with nasal stuffiness.

Bodily Itches

About a third of the love-shy are bothered by itches all over their bodies.

In fact, half of the love-shy men said they could not wear woolen items because it made them feel uncomfortable and itchy.

Shyness and the social aloneness it brings may effectively lower a person's resistance to allergies by raising the level of cortisol in the blood. While many people leave their allergies behind with childhood, for love-shy men allergies remain chronic, life-long problems.

Reactive Hypoglycemia

Another problem love-shy men suffer from is hypoglycemia, or low blood sugar, and its related problems of chronic fatigue, difficulty getting up in the morning, halitosis, hyperperspiration, hyperactive salivary glands and leg cramps.

Hypoglycemia is caused by the Isles of Langerhans in the pancreas secreting more insulin than the body requires, thus removing sugar from the blood stream and causing chronic fatigue and low physical energy. Forty-seven percent of the love-shy men complained of inertia, that feeling of somehow being powerless to remove the invisible chains that bind one to a boring life, compared to only 11 percent of the non-shy men. Even when they slept for seven hours, almost two-thirds of the love-shy men still had trouble getting up out of bed in the morning compared to only 17 percent of the socially self-confident. The love-shys usually required around 16 minutes to get up out of bed, compared to only 7.5 minutes for the non-shy men.

One third of my respondents were usually so tired after their last high school class that they were anxious to get home to take a nap. None of the non-shy men felt that way. Recent medical studies on high school teenagers have shown that young people who experience extreme tiredness by the end of the school day usually have reactive hypoglycemia and eat and drink a significant amount of high-sugar foods, such as soda, candy bars, cakes and pastries. This was also true of the love-shys. They recalled drinking an average of almost six cans of soda per week at the age of fifteen, compared to only about three cans per week for the non-shys.

Many of the love-shys had a strong penchant for sweet drinks involving milk and chocolate or malt. They averaged almost seven per week during their teens, compared to only about two such drinks per week for the non-shys. The love-shys estimated that they had eaten an average of 4.87 candy bars per week during their teens, while the average which the non-shy ate was only 2.21. The love-shys had long been in the habit of using quite a bit more sugar than the non-shys in their coffee and tea as well. The non-shys usually used just one teaspoonful per cup compared to two per cup for the love-shys.

The chronic fatigue and lethargy that are symptomatic of reactive hypoglycemia serve to reinforce love-shyness, by enabling the afflicted individual to feel justified in avoiding extracurricular and other social activities so that he can go home and rest. Hypoglycemia may represent one more way that normal social-emotional growth and development can be stunted.

In his recent work entitled *Stress-Free Living*, Dr. Clay Sherman commented on an experiment that had been conducted in an elite boarding school for high school students. Students who took part in this experiment were randomly assigned to one or the other of two groups. One group was given a heavy daily dose of malted milks, pastries, soda pop, candies and other high sugar foods, and the second ate low-sugar foods.

At the end of the academic year, the high-sugar group had a significantly lower proportion of students holding high student government offices. They were also poorer in interpersonal skills, grade-point average, concentration, relations with authority figures and athletic ability.

Thus, a high-sugar diet may represent a major variable interacting in synergy with other variables that gives rise to intractable love-shyness. Of course, young people may eat a lot of sugary foods as a substitute for the love, caring and concern that they are not getting from parents, peers and opposite-sexed age-mates.

Other Hypoglycemic Symptoms

Many of the shy young men often suffer from severe leg cramps, especially upon waking in the morning. In fact, such severe cramps painfully awaken some hypoglycemics in the middle of the night, causing them to rise and sit hard upon the calf of the leg. Severe leg cramps were three times more commonplace among the love-shys than they were among the non-shys.

Acid stomach is another fairly frequent side effect of hypoglycemia, and 33 percent of the love-shys suffered from this with considerable frequency. In contrast, only 12 percent of the non-shys had problems with acid stomach.

Halitosis is another widespread concomitant of reactive hypoglycemia. And better than two-fifths of the love-shys believed that they frequently had this problem, compared to only three percent of the non-shys.

Hyperactive Salivary Glands

Hypoglycemia causes some people to produce too much saliva—a problem which causes so many of the love-shys I interviewed to use an inordinate amount of kleenex. As an antidote, most love-shy men seem to drink unusually large amounts of water.

Most healthy people can simply poke a "life-saver" or a piece of hard candy into their mouths as a means of feeling more comfortable. Most love-shy people cannot seem to be able to do this without feeling severe fatigue, an uncomfortable feeling in their stomach, or a very bitterly unpleasant after-taste. Unfortunately, sugar-free breath pills seem to cause the same unpleasant effects for them.

One-fourth of the love-shy men were psychologically incapable of swallowing their own saliva, compared to only 5 percent of the non-shy men. And almost two-thirds of the love-shys indicated that they had to expectorate a great deal more frequently than most people. Only one-third of the non-shys indicated a frequent need to spit.

Hyperperspiration

People suffering from hypoglycemia often perspire a great deal. Better than 70 percent of the love-shys thought their underarm perspiration to be far heavier than most people's and more difficult to control. Exacerbating the problem is the love-shy man's allergic sensitivity to the various over-the-counter deodorants. Almost one-third found conventional deodorants to cause painful blisters in their armpits.

Depression

Depression often accompanies hypoglycemia; and almost two-thirds of the love-shys frequently felt depressed, whereas none of the non-shy men did. Depression, like severe shyness itself, is closely related to the amount of monoamine oxidase in the brain. Further, the fact that the brains of depressed people do not metabolize sugar anywhere nearly as efficiently or as effectively as do the brains of the non-depressed, may also have an important bearing upon the biochemistry of severe shyness or behavioral inhibition.

Shy people also tend to use a lot of salt on certain foods,

perhaps a reflection of overworked, overstressed adrenal glands. As we have seen, severely shy people tend to have a surfeit of adrenal-produced cortisol and norepinephrine in their bloodstreams.

Throat Clearing and Coughing

One of the characteristics that I have long noticed among shy men is that they tend to clear their throats and/or cough significantly more than anybody else. Almost three-fifths of the love-shys cleared their throats a lot, compared to less than one-fifth of the non-shy men.

Acne

None of the 500 men had serious skin problems when they were interviewed. However, it is well-known that a history of teenage acne often leaves mild to serious emotional scars. Thus, I deemed it appropriate to ask each man a question about acne problems that might have been suffered during adolescence. Not surprisingly, three out of every five of the love-shy men had had moderate to severe cases of acne during their teens. In contrast, this had been true for only one quarter of the self-confident, non-shy men.

There is some evidence suggesting that throughout their teens love-shy males tend to suffer from an excess of certain androgens, male sex hormones, which cause acne.

The fact that excess androgens are closely associated with acne ties in with a fascinating finding of University of London psychologist Hans Eysenck. Eysenck found that very shy people tend to have significantly stronger sex drives than non-shy people. He found that the stronger and more persistent a man's anxiety feelings tended to be, the stronger would be his sex drive and the more frequently he would feel the need to masturbate. As we saw in the last chapter, love-shy men tend to masturbate more frequently than the non-shy.

A cruel paradox is that severe acne serves to exacerbate teenage unpopularity with the opposite sex and increase self-consciousness and the self-defeating habit of social avoidance. But that acne is caused by the very same thing that causes heightened sexual interest, which cannot be fulfilled because of the acne and related shyness and social-self-consciousness.

Even though females have fewer androgens than males do, their androgens too cause acne and sexual arousal. Amusingly, those high school girls most desirous of erotic stimulation can often be spotted because they are the ones with the worst cases of acne.

Miscellaneous Sensitivities

Sensitivity to bright sunshine accounts for the tendency of some children to withdraw from certain types of outdoor activity. In American society this sort of sensitivity is of greater social harm to a boy than to a girl.

Sixty percent of the love-shys did not enjoy playing in bright sunlight as children. Almost three-fifths of the love-shys would like to live in a breezy climate where it never gets colder than 40 degrees Fahrenheit or hotter than 60 degrees Fahrenheit, compared to just 14 percent of the non-shys.

Fifty-seven percent of the love-shys and two percent of the non-shy men couldn't stand rough fingernails. The fact that the non-shys were less than one-twenty-fifth as likely as the love-shys to be bothered by a rough fingernail may partly reflect a greater ability on their part to lose themselves in the many activities in which they are involved. The ability to become lost in what one is doing is one index of mental health and happiness.

In the same vein, the squeaking of chalk on a blackboard did not bother 60 percent of the non-shys, but only 16 percent of the love-shys could say the same. While this might seem trivial, it is exactly the type of stimulus that invites bullying.

Fear of Pain in Medical Settings

One of the major earmarks of severe and chronic shyness is that it tends to be associated with a very low physical pain threshold as well as an unusually low anxiety threshold. The love-shy men are highly sensitive to physical pain and very fearful of experiencing it—a key reason, no doubt, why throughout their childhood years the love-shys avoided all rough and tumble play. The love-shys also tended to fear experiencing pain at the doctor's office. In view of the substantial number of medical problems from which the love-shys suffer, I found it interesting that they tended to visit doctors a good deal less often than the non-shys.

Forty-five percent of the love-shys would avoid having a strongly recommended (but not absolutely requiried) surgical procedure because of fear of pain, discomfort and being put to sleep. None of the non-shy men had that fear. Other fears also entered into the aversion to physicians and to medical facilities. Some fear they would scream in pain when other people are around. Others worry about being seen nude by nurses. Urinating and defecating constituted another anxiety. As one 24-year-old man said to me:

> I wouldn't have the nerve to go to the bathroom. I mean they make you use these bedpan things when you are confined to your bed. I'd never have the nerve to do that with the nurses and other people there! I think I'd go insane because of the horrible lack of privacy!

Some of the men recounted embarrassing scenes from childhood such as crying in pain on getting injections when other children, including girls, did not. The love-shys were often haunted by long-ago embarrassments to the point of being distracted from work or study.

One 37-year-old love-shy man told me about how he could remember jumping on tables and chairs in doctors' offices in order to avoid a shot. In fact, several of the love-shys recalled having to be held down by parents or medical staff, even when they reached the age of 14 or 15.

Several of the love-shys confessed that they break out in a cold sweat whenever they enter a physician's office. Love-shy men tend to be so nervous that the medical staff even comments on it.

One physician notes that whenever he administers the knee-jerk test to a particularly shy or fearful male, his leg will overreact, sometimes to an inordinate degree.

In sum, love-shy males tend to greatly fear pain and anxiety. And these fears sometimes keep them away from health-care delivery systems for inordinately long periods of time. Despite their many medical symptoms, most of the love-shy get medical examinations only when absolutely required.

Postscript

Pregnant women should be strongly advised to have their blood sugar metabolism checked and closely monitored. A 1988 *New England Journal of Medicine* article found faulty sugar metabolism in pregnant women to be associated with a high incidence of stillbirths and miscarriages. However, when women with blood sugar metabolism problems were closely monitored throughout their pregnancies, their babies were as healthy as those of women without blood sugar metabolism problems.

As was indicated in Chapter 5 of this book, love-shys' mothers tend to have an unusually high incidence of miscarriages and stillbirths. Further, a truculent, irascible disposition in women is itself known to be associated with sugar metabolism problems.

Hypoglycemia (see pages 138–139) in pregnant mothers may even constitute a direct cause of severe shyness. Thus, heavy carbohydrate consumption increases the concentration in the bloodstream of an amino acid called *tryptophan*—which permeates the blood-brain barrier very easily. Once in the brain, tryptophan converts to *serotonin*, a key neurotransmitter in the shyness/behavioral inhibition syndrome.

In addition, an excess of serotonin is now known to be heavily implicated in obsessive-compulsive disorders. As this book has shown, severely shy people tend to be afflicted from early childhood onward with many obsessive thoughts, tics, and compulsive behaviors. Such tendencies are among the factors that cause shys to become the targets of bullies. Incidentally, it is now known that the drug *clomipramine* (trade name is "*Anafranil*") will effectively regulate, for most people, serotonin imbalances.

Chapter 13

Therapy

There are four crucial components to any viable program of therapy for love-shy men. The first of these is appropriate pharmacological treatment which can be received through a licensed psychiatrist or neurologist. The second component is practice-dating therapy. The third component entails mental imaging and positive self-talk. And the fourth is active involvement in a meaningful and emotionally rewarding (quasi-kinship) support group.

All of the available evidence clearly demonstrates that love-shy men require strong catalysts if they are to lead more normal lives. Conventional counseling and psychotherapy waste time. And time is an extremely valuable resource when it comes to helping severely love-shy people. As love-shy men become older, they become decreasingly confident vis-a-vis attractive, eligible young women. For a love-shy man there is no more powerful therapy than being able to socialize with eligible young women.

"Crutches"

Conservative minds decry the idea of providing love-shy males with a "crutch." In psychotherapy, "crutches" are commonly thought to foster dependency. Yet in medicine crutches are known to speed the day when a person can function on his or her own unencumbered. Crutches also permit self-sufficiency, even as healing occurs.

A therapeutic crutch intrinsic in practice-dating therapy permits those incapacitated by severe love-shyness to exercise their limited interpersonal skills and develop viable social self-confidence.

Just as a seriously injured person is not expected to fend for himself until his broken bones heal, neither should a love-shy person be expected to fend for himself until he gets better. A competent physician takes the patient by the hand and starts him on certain regular exercises, which the patient eventually will do on his own. So it is with practice-dating therapy.

Pharmacological Treatment

For some victims of love-shyness, pharmacological treatment may be a *sine qua non*. This is why it is so important for all love-shys to be evaluated by a licensed physician specializing in psychiatry or neurology. Over the past 15 years the medical establishment has developed certain drugs which offer considerable hope for those suffering from social phobias including love-shyness. These drugs seem to prevent some people with social phobias from experiencing anxiety in social encounters. And they can serve as an effective catalyst enabling a person to derive far greater benefits than he otherwise would from the various cognitive and behavior modification-oriented forms of therapy in which he may be engaged. Of course, all such drugs must be prescribed and monitored by a licensed physician.

A drug that effectively lessens feelings of anxiety might prove useful as a preventive measure for conspicuously withdrawn, socially isolated, prepubescent youngsters; for shy young adolescents who want to date but cannot bring themselves to do it; and as an accompaniment to practice-dating therapy. However, as a sole method of therapy for love-shy people beyond the age of 15, I believe that drugs will fail to effect changes in social behavior or in social self-confidence. Even if a severely love-shy man could be guaranteed that he would not experience anxiety in the company of a woman, he would still be forced to deal with the formidable obstacles of inertia, anticipatory anxiety, and retrospective anxiety.

Practice-Dating Therapy

Practice-dating is a form of behavior therapy oriented towards extinguishing inappropriate anxieties and fears. Traditionally, behavior therapy entailed bringing the person face-to-face with the thing that he most strongly feared. Conventional shyness clinics and assertiveness training seminars often assign a nervous and inhibited man to approach and start a conversation with a woman who interests him. But, the vast majority of severely love-shy men will not cooperate in any exercise that arouses too much painful anxiety or even the fear of experiencing painful anxiety which is known as anticipatory anxiety. The vast majority of severely love-shy men find it extremely anxiety-provoking to even visualize themselves making a friendly overture to a young woman. Inasmuch as it requires very little to painfully arouse the very low native anxiety threshold of a love-shy man, the task of engineering workable therapeutic programs has not been easy.

Nevertheless, my work with love-shy males has convinced me that almost all of them will cooperate when someone else takes the responsibility of arranging introductions on their behalf. This is especially true if these arranged introductions are followed by a program of structured activities in which the love-shy men are not made to feel emotionally threatened in any way.

Practice-dating therapy requires the client to date a woman his own age, in a match arranged by therapeutic staff. It is the responsibility of each client to go out on the dates and to attend twice-weekly 90-minute group sessions per week during which the men discuss anxieties and problems and participate in such structured exercises as psychodrama, role playing, group visualization, mental imaging and mental rehearsal.

The most effective practice-dating programs incorporate two 90-minute group sessions per week for six men and six women. Each meeting is led by one and sometimes two clinical psychologists, occasionally aided by one or two clinical psychology graduate students. The therapy is conducted in an office that is large enough to comfortably accommodate the 12 clients and the therapeutic staff. Folding chairs are placed in a circle so that everybody is facing each other. Tables are not employed as these impede full vision. Each member of the group must be able to clearly see every other member; men and women alternate around the circle.

Toward the conclusion of each 90-minute session, the group leader assigns each of the 12 group members to a person of the opposite sex. During the early weeks of therapy this person selected by the therapist will be a fellow client from within the group. Each must go out on a date with his preselected partner before the next meeting for a minimum of two hours. They can do anything they want except go to the movies, watch television, study together—activities that might discourage conversation.

The participants are told that silent periods probably will develop during the dates, that they are normal and nothing to worry about. During later therapeutic meetings, the shys learn a variety of relaxation and meditation techniques to lessen tension which makes it difficult to think of things to talk about, blocking the creative flow of ideas.

The love-shy male finds it quite easy to arrange the date because he has met the girl at the meeting, and she expects him to call.

At the next biweekly 90-minute therapy meeting, each of the 12 members will discuss his experiences on his practice date. Participants are encouraged to be frank during these sessions so that everyone can learn where his strengths and weaknesses lie. Much of the time during each therapy meeting is devoted to training in better interpersonal skills, grooming, posture, poise and speech patterns. Video-tape cameras and play-back VCRs figure prominently as do psychodrama and role playing.

Towards the end of the session, the therapist again pairs up each client. This time the clients are paired with a different member of the opposite sex. Before the next meeting, each participant is expected to meet with his assigned date for a two-hour outing. This same procedure is followed for each meeting.

During the early weeks of the program, each love-shy man

gets to know the six women in his group. If more than one practice-dating group is operating simultaneously, each client is supplied with a list of the participants. Love-shy men often phone women on the list, indicating that the experience of going out on assigned dates effectively extinguishes many anxieties.

About the sixth week of the practice-dating regimen, the therapist specifically assigns each male client the exercise of phoning a female member of another practice-dating group for a date. By this time this therapeutic exercise usually arouses little anxiety. He has already dated each of the six girls in his own group two or three times; and he knows that the girls in the other groups are going to be as open to his call as the girls in his own group.

Every six or seven weeks dances are held for members of all the practice-dating groups with required attendance. Particularly inhibited men are accorded special attention there by the therapeutic staff to help diminish shyness-related anxieties.

The therapist makes clear at the outset of practice-dating therapy that clients are not expected to fall in love with or develop any lasting romantic commitments to their practice-dating partners. Of course, if a romantic interest does develop so much the better. The purpose of practice-dating is to enable love-shys to get to know and appreciate the opposite sex as thinking, feeling human beings like themselves. Practice-dating is further intended to remove false illusions about the other sex; illusions which promote separateness, mutual suspicion and non-interaction.

The belief that only conspicuously attractive women are worth getting to know is one of the most destructive and self-limiting of these illusions. Love-shy men learn that women of only average looks often turn out to be charming and worth knowing.

Self-consciousness about personal attractiveness is dealt with during the group meetings. For example, discussions focus on personal grooming, hair style, dress, posture. But more importantly, the positive mental attitudes and enhanced self-confidence that the therapeutic regimen promotes also serve to significantly enhance the physical attractiveness of all practice-dating participants. It certainly is true that people look better when they feel positive about themselves. This, in turn, helps to fire them with enthusiasm about life. Practice-dating serves to accomplish these goals.

Of crucial importance is the fact that people tend to learn some important things about themselves when they begin to interact regularly with other people, particularly with those of the opposite sex. This is why love-shy men commonly experience an almost religious awakening when they learn to enjoy being with someone who at first seems physically unattractive. As these love-shy men begin to perceive physical beauty, they also begin relishing richness in the personalities of the women they are dating. This is important because it is on the basis of personality that most emotionally mature, well-adjusted people select their marriage partners.

Recruitment of Female Participants

If advertisements for practice-dating therapeutic services are posted only on college and university campuses, the number of men greatly exceed the number of women. Therefore, other methods must be employed to attract female participants. Three approaches have been found to be especially useful in this regard: recruiting women who are interested in upgrading their social self-confidence, with no mention in promotional material regarding shyness with the opposite sex; recruiting women from local-area high schools; and recruiting young women who attend neither high school nor college.

Young women attending various types of assertiveness-training seminars, shyness clinics, and group therapy sessions could be convinced that practice-dating groups constitute loyal and cohesive support groups in which they might establish loyal friendships with people of both sexes. In addition, practice-dating group meetings are highly effective in upgrading assertiveness skills and social self-confidence. Satisfied female participants and graduates of practice-dating groups could be paid to deliver brief promotional talks before various groups of young women and girls.

As for the second point, university-based practice-dating programs should make good use of local area high schools since most men prefer women who are a few years their junior. This is especially true for love-shy men, most of whom have an above-average need for a woman partner who will look up to them.

Finally, radio and newspaper ads could be developed to attract young women from the community not attending school. The interest of psychotherapists throughout the community could also be aroused. They might thus be in a position to recommend the practice-dating experience for their young women clients.

Psychodrama and Role Playing

Much of each 90-minute period in practice-dating therapy will be devoted to psychodrama in which the therapist presents the group with a scenario that might arouse anxiety in a shy couple. The therapist describes a scene and asks the woman to play the person in whom the love-shy man has a strong romantic interest. The two people then improvise for about ten minutes. Occasionally, the therapist asks a man to play a girl and vice-versa. The exercise is video-taped and played back later so that the participants can review it, and other group members can more easily make constructive suggestions.

Psychodrama is an extremely powerful therapeutic device, allowing people to experience what it feels like to be in another person's shoes. The procedure teaches compassion and understanding of others, at the same time enhancing self-knowledge.

There is a process in successful interpersonal relationships which sociologists call role taking. Role taking is not the same thing as role playing. In role taking a person tries to "feel for" the other person, anticipating the thoughts and feelings of his partner while the informal interaction is proceeding. Generally speaking, the better a person becomes at role taking, the easier it becomes for him to move the relationship in the direction of his choosing. The other person feels safe and secure with someone who trusts and respects his feelings, needs and wishes. And he comes to want to do what the other desires.

In psychodrama, participants learn both role taking and role playing. When the exercises are carried out in a supportive, non-competitive setting, as in practice-dating therapy, people come to grips with what they are doing wrong and learn to improve their performance. Thus, the exercises gradually improve the social self-confidence and social finesse of group members vis-a-vis the opposite sex.

The "Second Plateau"

There are basically two plateaus that must be overcome in love-shyness. The first has to do with launching a relationship with a woman. The second plateau has to do with being able to relax and to communicate naturally and sincerely with a person one hopes to get to know well. Most love-shy men devote the first four or five dates to superficial small talk limited to such topics as their educational majors, careers, family, hobbies, preferences in music and television. After they run out of superficial topics, love-shy men typically stop seeing a woman they really care about because there are too many uncomfortable silences. Practice-dating therapy helps people get over this second plateau by making them interact with a variety of assigned women. Practice-dating fosters an increased ability to relax in the company of women, to be oneself, and to perceive women of varying levels of attractiveness as being non-anxiety-provoking, non-threatening human beings just like themselves.

But practice-dating itself is not enough. This is why a variety of exercises involving visualization and mental imagery are used to help love-shy men learn to make physical displays of affection.

Make no mistake about it! Such physical displays are *normatively prescribed* in our culture after a certain number of dates have transpired with the same woman. And a woman will very seldom feel comfortable about accepting additional dates with a man who does not respond to these normative prescriptions. Indeed, she is quite likely to begin *wrongly* perceiving such a shy and inhibited man as being a "latent homosexual". As she cannot understand him, "latent homosexual" seems to be a logical enough label to apply to him—even though it is a quite false label.

In American society we tend to be so preoccupied with the far more typical male behavior of "moving too fast" with a woman, that we tend to neglect the fact that men who "move too slowly" with a woman (for other than overtly stated and mutually shared religious reasons) *also violate norms*. And these normative violations are often a good deal more difficult for a woman to deal with than the "moving too fast" type of violation. Most young women have received a good deal of socialization from both peers and parents about ways of successfully dealing with the excessively "fast mover". Never having received any socialization about ways of dealing with the excessively "slow mover", the typical woman tends to become confused, worried and upset. Again, people tend to most strongly fear those things (behaviors *and behavioral omissions*) which they have never been prepared to understand.

Visualization and Mental Rehearsal

The love-shy client is asked to mentally rehearse informal social interactions with desired women. Thus, the love-shy man sees himself actively engaged in pleasant conversation with an attractive woman. He both sees and feels himself to be relaxed and comfortable. And he sees himself handling the situation in a way the woman finds charming. Research data support the efficacy of visualization. For example, a large number of junior-high-school boys of relatively equal athletic ability were randomly sorted into three separate groups. The boys in the first group practiced basketball free throws one hour each morning for a month. Their accuracy rate shot up to 46 percent. The boys in the second group spent one hour each day for a month visualizing themselves making basketball free throws, with 100 percent accuracy. At the end of the month, their accuracy rate had shot up to 44 percent—almost as high as the accuracy rate of the boys who had actually been practicing free throws. The boys in the third group engaged in both types of practice. They made free throws for an hour a day. And they also spent one hour each day visualizing themselves making basketball free throws with complete accuracy. At the end of the month, this group achieved a 66 percent accuracy.

Simply put, if a love-shy man actively participates in a regular set of programmed visualizations in which he sees himself involved in successful pursuit as well as participating in real dating, the beneficial effects are multiplied.

A basic precept of behavior therapy is that the physiological and neurological mechanisms of the human body cannot tell the difference between the actual experience and the imagined experience. Visualization exercises have a long and distinguished history as a viable therapeutic modality. Today many major sports and entertainment figures practice it. In fact, visualization exercises go back as far as ancient Egypt.

In practice-dating therapy programs, visualization exercises tend to be most effective when practiced in the early morning on arising and just before going to bed at night. Clients are asked to pair up with each other to catalyze each other's efforts toward visualization and meditation exercises. One member induces the other into a light meditative trance. He reads quietly from a five-by-eight-inch card to the person in a trance. The scenario usually involves approaching or talking to a girl with whom the subject has long wanted to make social contact.

Since these sessions usually last between 20 minutes and half an hour, only one person can receive help at a session. Thus, if client "A" is the recipient during the morning meditation session, during the evening session the roles will be reversed and client "A" will help client "B". Eventually clients should be able to do visualization and mental rehearsal exercises on their own. But the support group must be on hand if members ask for help.

In sum, a person tends to become what he thinks about. Visualization exercises entailing friendly, assertive behavior towards young women substantially facilitate improvements caused by the practice-dating itself. Practice-dating and mental rehearsal operate in synergistic interaction to catalyze rapid psychoemotial and social growth in love-shy men. Visualization exercises also help extinguish anxiety reactions.

Group Exercises

Visualized goals tend to take on formidable power for the good when the visualization is shared with a group. For example, all the group members might agree that every night from 10:00 until 10:10 they will stop whatever they are doing and intensely visualize a particular desired outcome for a predesignated group member. Or they might simultaneously visualize the person they are trying to help being suffused by a powerful white light. Each group member would receive his/her turn on different occasions. This procedure can be followed even if one of the group members happens to be spending a few nights in another time zone by adjusting the exercise time accordingly.

Systematic visualization is simply an issue of "mind over matter." It is a form of psychokinesis ("PK"), sometimes called "telekinesis". All matter including the human body is simply a form of energy that is vibrating at comparatively low rates. The concerted effort of, for example, eleven people all simultaneously focusing on the same goal, appears to do much to cause that goal to come to pass.

Many highly successful business people swear by systematic visualization. Amidst a group wherein success is measured almost entirely by monetary profit, it seems highly unlikely that systematic visualization would be dealt with at all if it did not demonstrate an impressive history of yielding positive, measurable results. Thought is a powerful energy form.

Systematic visualization exercises which can be easily incorporated into practice-dating therapy programs include the following:

(1) For ten minutes at an agreed upon time each night each of the twelve members of a practice-dating group intensely visualizes in his/her mind's eye a particular fellow member happily and successfully making love with a member of the opposite sex. This visualization must be strongly felt and believed as well as seen and heard in the mind's eye and ear. The recipient of the exercise for a particular evening must simultaneously be involved in the visualization as well—on his or her own behalf.

(2) For ten minutes each night each group member sees in his/her mind's eye a powerful pale of red light suffusing the entire body, and especially the brain, of a preselected group memeber. Red is the color of energy in occult studies. And love-shy people are often highly discouraged and bogged down in the throes of psychoemo-

tional enertia. Red light is therefore appropriate. After the red light is used for a while, the group may also use a powerful pale of green light to bring peace and freedom from anxiety to the person.

(3) Each of the twelve members of a therapy group will be encouraged to systematically visualize on his/her own behalf at several different times each day. Each member will be asked to both see and feel himself/herself to be exactly the person he/she wishes to become—particularly in reference to happy and successful man-woman interaction. Thus, the all-powerful self-image deeply imbedded in the subconscious mind gradually comes to be reprogrammed. People tend to move towards becoming that which they intensely see, feel, hear, and believe in their mind's eye and ear.

Positive Self-Talk

We all talk to ourselves endlessly. This is one reason why meditation is so difficult for most adults to learn. Meditation is difficult because it requires stilling and quieting the conscious mind to the point where self-talk stops. It requires bypassing the personal ego to the point at which the subconscious mind can be reached.

Thought tends to create form, and we tend to become that which we think about most of the time. A key common denominator of the pathologically love-shy is negative self-talk. As they do not have friends to distract negative thinking patterns, their self-talk tends to be more constant than for other negative thinkers.

Hence, an important component of therapy for the love-shy is a reversal of these negative self-talk habits and tendencies. Practice-dating programs can accomplish a great deal just from the standpoint of distracting a love-shy man from his negative thinking habits. If we do indeed tend to become what we think about, it is clear that negative self-talk must be replaced by positive self-talk. The love-shy must be reprogrammed to replace negative faith with positive faith.

A love-shy person also needs a support group to help him replace his negative self-talk. These groups help him muster the necessary self-discipline and ego strength for accomplishing necessary exercises.

The first step in mastering positive self-talk is learning and using positive self-affirmations. Successful business people studied by behavioral scientists have this key element in common: better than 90 percent of them frequently use positive self-affirmations and self-talk.

The way we talk to ourselves serves as a major way whereby the subconscious mind (which is very much like a computer) gets programmed. The subconscious mind constitutes a kind of automatic pilot in the life of any human being. To the extent that it is programmed negatively, the person moves toward negative, unhappy experiences as a form of self-fulfilling prophecy. In this respect the conscious, intellectual mind is of far less consequence in a person's life than is his subconscious mind.

The following are examples of positive self-affirmations which the severely love-shy might practice as self-talk:

1. I am very successful with women.
2. I am God as a companion to women.
3. Attractive women compete for my companionship.
4. I am a happy-go-lucky person with a much appreciated sense of humor.
5. I am deeply and sincerely loved by a woman who matters greatly to me.
6. Women respond in a positive, friendly manner to all of my friendly overtures.
7. I am God as a conversationalist vis-a-vis attractive women.
8. I am an excellent conversationalist with women.
9. I am relaxed and completely able to enjoy myself whenever I am in the company of women.
10. I am God in my ability to meet and to befriend the right people.
11. I am God in my ability to assert myself in a friendly, courteous manner whenever I am around women.
12. Women enjoy being in my company.

For those self-talk affirmations beginning with "I am God," I took my cue from Shirley MacLaine's discussion in her book entitled *Dancing in the Light*. Some readers might object to this phraseology; but for those who can abide it, this wording can work wonders.

It is extremely important that the love-shy condition themselves to stop their thoughts in their tracks whenever they catch themselves engaging in negative self-talk. Again, self-talk (whether positive or negative) programs the robot computer of the subconscious mind to create a self-image that is life-governing. A positive self-image leads to healthy outcomes whereas a negative self-image tends to produce trouble and failure for a person.

Because it is difficult for love-shy men to get into the habit of controlling their thoughts in a positive direction, cassette programs have been devised that can be played during a person's free moments. It is just when a person is relatively free of responsibility and in a state of reverie that self-talk normally wields its deepest impact on the shaping of the subconscious self-image. In self-image therapy, the shy client is asked to play a positive self-talk cassette as often as possible, especially during the first several months of therapy.

There are two types of self-talk cassettes: subliminal and audible. The latter remain by far the most commonplace. However, subliminal tapes have been found by many to be highly effective. On such tapes the only things the listener hears are either ocean waves or soft music. Tapes with the sounds of ocean waves are especially useful as they can be played at any time, no matter what the listener is doing.

There are four audible self-talk audio-cassette programs that I particularly recommend. The first is Shad Helmstetter's self-talk audio-cassette series which is published by the Grindle Press of Scottsdale, Arizona. Thses cassettes are available through regular bookstores.

Perhaps the best program currently available is Jonathan Parker's *Build a Winning Self-Image* and *Prosperity Solution* tapes. This program includes both audible and subliminal self-talk cassettes as well as a great deal of valuable instructional material. It is available through Nightengale-Conant Corporation of Chicago.

The third and fourth programs I wish to recommend are also published by Nightengale-Conant, and are by Denis E. Waitley. The first of these is called *The Inner Winner*, and the second program, more instructional in nature, is called *The Psychology of Winning*.

In *The Inner Winner*, Waitley recommends that clients make their own self-talk audio-cassettes by reading one's list of self-talk affirmations while simultaneously playing recordings of Johann Sebastian Bach as background music. Bach's music in the background has been found to quite substantially facilitate the internalization of self-talk affirmations to the subconscious mind. Waitley's program contains plentiful samples of music and a large array of positive self-talk affirmations.

The Alcoholics Anonymous Model of Mutual Caring and Concern

One of the key goals of therapy is to make the therapeutic group a cohesive unit and, indeed, a kind of quasi-kin group that will provide emotional support for its fellow members when they are in need. Thus, the third crucial ingredient of an effective practice-dating program is for the therapy groups to be patterned after Alcoholics Anonymous support groups.

Same-sexed members of support groups are encouraged to see each other outside meetings and help each other with problems that crop up. For example, when a man fails to show up for a meeting, a fellow male member is asked to check up on the missing person and encourage him to make a date or do whatever it is he is avoiding.

On some campuses, the graduates of practice-dating are so enthusiastic about the program that they agree to help new practice-dating clients. Alcoholics Anonymous encourages such friendships between experienced and inexperienced members, believing it to be a prime factor in its success in keeping members from drinking.

Like many other social nonconformists, love-shy people tend to have a long history of little or no kin-group support. People with such a history tend to benefit in important ways from becoming members of quasi-kin groups that are apropos to their needs and interests. The membership of the 12-person practice-dating therapy groups can and should be made to function as caring social support and friendship groups.

No Time Limit

One of the most important virtues of practice-dating therapy is that there are no time limits to it. If a client appears to be suffering from a particularly intractable case of love-shyness, he is made to feel free about remaining with the program for as long as he chooses. Regardless of whether a person remains in therapy for a brief period of time or for a long period of time, the principle of extinction remains the dynamic whereby destructive inhibitions and anticipatory anxieties are gradually relinquished. A small minority of men, especially older love-shys, have to practice-date scores of women before they become disinhibited enough to loosen up and contact women on their own. Everybody has his own internal clock or timetable, and a therapist shouldn't give up on a person simply because he is taking a long time to display meaningful growth and progress.

Of course, the therapeutic regimen is not permissive. All participants must go out on all assigned dates, attend group meetings, participate in exercises there and do homework. But practice-dating clients are never asked to do anything that is beyond their psychoemotional ability to handle.

Further, practice-dating therapy trains its participants to be responsible to some extent for each other. As in Alcoholics Anonymous, people who had made progress are encouraged to make friends with and to look in on less experienced and still somewhat frightened practice-dating participants. The idea is to make the newer participants feel as though people care about their welfare.

Exceptionally Stubborn Cases

The only men who cannot be cured by the practice-dating experience are those who cannot or will not do the assigned exercises. All told, this comes to less than five percent of those who enter practice-dating groups. However, there are certain men—about 15 percent of those who enter practice dating—who never seem to reach the point where they become emotionally capable of approaching women for dates on their own.

If these men remain in practice-dating therapy long enough, they fall in love with women from different practice-dating groups. Typically when this happens it occurs six months to one year after practice-dating therapy has commenced.

When a genuinely mutual love relationship develops, the man is given the option of either remaining in therapy until the therapeutic goal of self-sufficiency has been achieved or of dropping out and pursuing a monogamous courtship relationship with his chosen. If he chooses the second option, and about 75 percent of love-shy men do, he can return for either one-on-one or group treatment if he feels the need at any time in the future. For if a man falls in love with and marries one of his assigned practice-dates, therapy has been successful. And if a severely love-shy man is patient and remains actively involved in practice-dating long enough, he will eventually meet someone he wants to marry.

Notes

Regarding the making of affirmations, several therapists of late have commented on the effectiveness of simply standing before the bathroom mirror immediately upon arising in the morning, and just shouting out loud to one's reflection twenty to thirty times: "*I like myself! I like myself! I like myself!* etc." To be sure, this sounds like a very silly thing to do. However, those who can muster the self-discipline to regularly practice this exercise, particularly upon arising and again upon leaving for work or school, will find that it is a formidable morale booster and that it has a cumulative, beneficial impact upon level of self-esteem. This exercise can be especially powerful when members of a support group, as in practice-dating, come in and take turns overseeing each other doing it.

Chapter 14

Some Recommendations Concerning Careers for Love-Shys

The experience of interviewing hundreds of people has convinced me that there are certain steps which the love-shy can take that will minimize the difficulties they are likely to encounter in their careers. My recommendations are applicable primarily to young people who are still in school. Parents, teachers and advisors of love-shy men will be able to be of special service to love-shys if they reflect carefully upon the following points.

First, love-shy young men need clearly established, realistic career goals. And the earlier in life they are able to commit themselves to these goals, the better off they are likely to be. It is not enough that the love-shy be able to visualize themselves attaining these goals, although that is important. What is most important is that these goals, once attained, permit life-long, stable careers.

Among the older love-shys who were interviewed for this book, few had given any serious thought to what kind of work they would engage in as adults. The younger love-shys were scarcely any better off in this regard. Most love-shy men had labored under the false notion that if they merely completed a university degree, they would be alright. Indeed, the saddest cases of all were men who had completed an M.S., M.A., or a Ph.D.

As we have seen, the love-shy tend to follow the law of least resistance in almost everything they do. And this is doubtless a key reason why they experience so many stumbling blocks in arriving at some semblance of success and happiness. The first mistake most of them make is choosing an academic major. Here the love-shy veer toward those fields which are most interesting to them and easiest to get good grades in.

A cardinal rule for love-shy men is this: The choice of a major is of infinitely greater importance than grade-point average. Good grades can be helpful. But the courses in which such grades are earned is a matter of far greater importance than the good grades themselves. Completion of a major in a technical field with a "C" average will very likely get a love-shy man a much better career opportunity than will an "A" average in a non-technical discipline that is not clearly related to the job market.

Some areas of employment require much greater social self-confidence than others do. Generally speaking, the greater the amount of technical knowledge that is required for entrance into a career field, the less self-confidence and interpersonal finesse that field is likely to require. Contrariwise, the smaller the amount of technical training and knowledge a field requires, the more that field is likely to demand in terms of interpersonal finesse and social self-confidence. Love-shy men who major in technical fields and develop salable skills adjust to their adult lives a great deal better than do love-shys who major in the liberal arts, social science, education and humanities disciplines. Therefore, the love-shy college student who feels that he must take some of these liberal arts courses should attend college a fifth year so that he can complete his technical degree.

A socially self-confident person need not be anywhere nearly so careful. Such a person can emerge from his university training with a "C" average and a degree in English or psychology or geography and end up making $30,000 or more in his second full year of employment—for example, in some sales capacity.

There is no shortage of sales career opportunities. But these jobs require individuals who are naturally sociable, relaxed, socially self-confident, high on interpersonal finesse, high on positive mental attitude and unusually insensitive to interpersonal anxiety. Most love-shy men without some form of technical training eventually end up working in commission sales for brief periods of time. And inevitably these experiences prove traumatic and emotionally harrowing for them.

Love-shy men simply do not possess the charm, polish and finesse necessary to get hired for white-collar career positions that are salaried and do not require a technical degree. To find such positions, the applicant must be hooked into a social network and have friends and/or relatives who are willing to speak on his behalf. As the data in this book have made painfully clear, love-shys have few or no friendships, and their kinship networks similarly tend to be very weak.

To be sure, young men occasionally find good, entry level career opportunities through newspaper job ads. However, in such cases the employment interviewer will almost always opt for the charming, handsome, well-groomed young man who appears naturally friendly, relaxed, sociable and spontaneous. The love-shy young man simply cannot compete—not even if his university grade-point average is superior to that of the sociable charmers who are accorded the better opportunities. The net upshot of all this is that love-shy men need a salable technical skill which will effectively permit them to compensate for deficits in their personality and looks.

On Selling an Employment Interviewer

To be sure, people with liberal arts degrees occasionally find business-related career opportunities outside the fields of sales and marketing. But this is actually very rare. In contrast, the person trained in accounting, finance, engineering, etc., has a solid skill to sell.

A person without technical training depends more heavily on the power and charm of his personality to win and to keep employment opportunities. The love-shy tend to lack both the power and the charm as well as the physical attractiveness instrumental in motivating an employment interviewer to think twice about them. Moreover, the severely love-shy is normally so emotionally incapable of even trying to seek an employer that he ends up making no attempts at all.

This is why severely love-shy, college educated men without technical training almost always end up underemployed. They end up in lower level clerical positions and as cab drivers, door-to-door canvassers, etc. Such unstable and disappointing employment situations serve to lower the love-shys' self-esteem to an ever worse degree. Such positions similarly serve to further reduce the love-shys' chances of ever meeting appropriate women.

The Importance of Being in Demand

Rugged individualists often delight in reminding us of a statement which the playwright George Bernard Shaw once made. In effect, "the people who get on in this world are those who are constantly on the lookout for new opportunities; and when they cannot find them they create their own opportunities." No evidence has ever been presented suggesting that love-shy men are any less intelligent than the rest of us. Indeed, many love-shys have no shortage of creative ideas. The problem is that they do not have the nerve to do and say the things which their God-given native intelligence tells them to do and say.

This is why it is of the utmost importance for love-shy men to take whatever steps may be necessary to be in demand from a career standpoint. Meaningful and enjoyable work represents one way to infuse enthusiasm into their lives. A job also provides some semblance of a social life. Involvement in meaningful, well-paid work can do much to bolster a person's overall self-esteem. And it can further serve to increase even a severely love-shy man's romantic chances.

Because of their thin-skinned, low anxiety thresholds, it is simply not realistic to expect severely love-shy men to "create their own opportunities" when the going gets tough. And this is why in counseling severely love-shy men, I always strongly emphasize the desirability—indeed the necessity—of their choosing and completing a college major which will place their services in demand in the labor market. Since love-shys are not emotionally capable of hustling, they must be prepared to sell their technical knowledge. And that technical knowledge must be in demand now and in the forseeable future.

In this regard, love-shys owe it to themselves to get the objective facts regarding job trends in areas of specialized career endeavor that they are considering. City libraries, university placement bureaus, and personnel agencies can provide helpful hints. So can major daily newspapers of the metropolitan area in which one hopes to reside. The greater the number of ads that appear for a particular occupation or career category, the safer that occupational or career category will prove for the love-shy individual.

Chapter 15

Some Final Thoughts on Prevention

It is far simpler and cheaper to prevent severe, chronic shyness from ever developing than it is to provide effective therapy. Thus, the most compassionate, moral, and cost-effective thing any of us can do with respect to this problem is to learn as much as we can about viable modes of prevention and put these methods into actual practice.

Highly Recommended Resources

Anyone who is truly sincere about preventing severe shyness in children, especially parents and teachers, should read and study the following books:

1. *The Shy Child: A Parent's Guide to Overcoming and Preventing Shyness from Infancy to Adulthood,* by Philip G. Zimbardo, and Shirley L. Radl. Published by Doubleday/Dolphin, in 1982. This book contains the best statement I've ever seen of the things that parents and teachers can do to effectively prevent shyness. The suggestions are all research-based and sensible. (NOTE: This book

171

is *not* to be confused with Zimbardo's earlier 1977 work entitled *Shyness, What It Is and What to Do About It*—which I do *not* recommend.)

2. *Know Your Child*, by Stella Chess and Alexander Thomas. Published in 1987, by Basic Books. Even a child born with the behavioral inhibition gene need never become shy. This research-based work explains why and how.

3. *Parent Effectiveness Training*, by Thomas Gordon. Published in 1970, by Wyden Books. This is the single, best methodological statement ever published of how to rear a happy, healthy child.

4. *P.E.T. in Action*, by Thomas Gordon. Published in 1976, by Wyden Books, this work presents a highly useful elaboration and clarification of the "PET" concepts.

5. *The One Minute Father*, by Spencer Johnson. Published in 1983, by William Morrow. This is a 112-page statement worth its weight in gold. It should be carefully studied and reflected upon. Toward this end I also highly recommend the two cassette tapes of the same title that were published by the Nightengale-Conant Corporation of Chicago.

6. *The One Minute Mother*, by Spencer Johnson, and also published in 1983, by William Morrow. You should choose either *The One Minute Father* or *The One Minute Mother*, and get the cassette tapes as well as the book. The two works present exactly the same enormously valuable material.

7. *What Do You Really Want for Your Children*, by Wayne Dyer. Published in 1985, by William Morrow. Nightengale-Conant cassette tapes also available for this title. The reader should note that I do not endorse Dyer's ideas for therapy. But I think his ideas for prevention are terrific!

8. *The Neuropsychology of Successful Parenting*, by Katherine C. Kersey. This is an audiocassette program which was published in 1986, by SyberVision Systems of Newark, California. The ten principles elaborated upon in this program are well-worth careful study and reflection. Despite its $70 price tag, this program is a must.

9. *Shyness and Love: Causes, Consequences and Treatment*, by Brian G. Gilmartin, and published in 1987, by University Press of America. This 701-page work contains a wealth of information.

Coed Scouts

I recommend a new nationwide (eventually worldwide) children's recreational organization called "Coed Scouts." This organization would serve as a bona-fide alternative to such well-established, traditional children's organizations as Cub Scouts, Brownies, Boy Scouts, Girl Scouts, Campfire Girls, YWCA, YMCA, Boys Club of America and Girls Club of America, where children are segregated by gender. I believe that this traditional practice is counterproductive in our contemporary, coeducational world particularly for socially-isolated and behaviorally-inhibited young boys.

Satisfactory adjustment in adulthood absolutely requires an ability to get along smoothly and harmoniously with both sexes. Boys who are shy and withdrawn with members of their own sex in elementary school are almost always afflicted with incipient love-shyness. Such boys would benefit enormously from membership in an organization comprised of equal numbers of girls and boys.

From the time children reach the age of two, American parents begin taking steps to encourage their children to play in gender-segregated peer groups, and to develop friendships exclusively with individuals of their own gender. Yet research evidence has shown that most young children do not naturally gravitate exclusively towards playmates of their own sex. In fact, if left entirely to their own devices, a majority of children will choose to play in coeducational peer groups.

I believe that the easy availability to all children who want it of a coeducational peer group would represent an extremely useful preventive device for heterosexual love-shyness. Coeducational Scouting organizations might be a godsend for boys with a passive, behaviorally inhibited temperament, who emotionally need intimate heterosexual interaction. Units of the Coed Scouts could be established which cross-cut school districts so that in the unlikely event that not enough boys from one district wish to join, there would always be a sufficient number of pre-love-shy boys from surrounding districts to fill the gap.

The little boy who will eventually develop into a young man so severely shy vis-a-vis girls that he cannot date or marry can easily be spotted in kindergarten and in the first grade. And inasmuch as he can be readily spotted, failure to take positive action to stem the tide of his ever worsening love-shyness is both unnecessary, unethical, and immoral.

Coed Scouting groups could be organized and led by interested adults (parents, teachers, etc.) in the community. However, these adults must be flexible, androgynous in their gender-role attitudes and values and be well-educated, particularly in the areas of child and adolescent development, personality, developmental psychology, learning theory, etc.

The Principle of the Superordinate Goal

A well established principle in the social sciences states that whenever two people cooperate toward the completion of some task important to both, the people will come to like and understand each other: and their values, attitudes and goals will tend to become increasingly similar. This is known as the principle of the superordinate goal. And it would seem to me to be particularly applicable to the problem of dispelling bashfulness and social timidity between an elementary school boy and girl who may have an interest in each other.

One of the prime benefits of active involvement in Coed Scouting is that there would be ample opportunity for adult leaders to provide boy-girl pairs with superordinate goals to work towards in a cooperative, friendly way. Even boys without sisters would thus be accorded the opportunity to develop interpersonal skills and social self-confidence. Over several years of informal, relaxed involvement in such social groups even the most behaviorally-inhibited children would be able to socialize and enjoy life as fully and as naturally as the more genetically-advantaged, extroverted children.

The Importance of Having a Support Group

Love-shy people tend to go through life without any meaningful or caring support group. This is as true for love-shy children as it is for love-shy adults. As I have stressed throughout this book, love-shy males of all ages tend to be social isolates. They tend to lack friends; and their families typically either don't care about them or have given up on them. In many cases their fathers and mothers are also severely lacking in interpersonal skills and social self-confidence—and as a consequence they too are socially isolated.

In Chapter 13, I made it clear that meaningful involvement in a caring support group constitutes one of the four indispensable components of therapy for love-shy individuals. Such involvement in a caring support group is equally important for the more important task of prevention. If severe love-shyness is to be successfully prevented, then all children must be assured daily involvement, including full membership in a meaningful, caring and emotionally rewarding friendship support group. The fact that love-shys seldom have a well integrated kinship network available to them as a support group renders it all the more important that they be deeply involved in a caring friendship support group at all times.

Coed Scouting groups can provide such caring friendship support groups. Indeed, under the right adult leadership, Coed Scouting can be modeled on the quasi-kinship support groups of Alcoholics Anonymous. AA is a quasi-kinship support group composed of people who come to care deeply about each other, almost as family. That is why it is successful and why it works so well. I have shown how and why practice-dating therapy groups can be and should be modeled after AA where each member genuinely views each fellow member as an important individual and true friend. The same thing applied to Coed Scouting groups would serve as a highly effective key to the prevention of love-shyness.

In order for Coed Scouts to function successfully as a support group, it must offer the right recreational activities. It must not revolve around highly competitive sports or games or strenuous physical exercises that are likely to frighten away love-shy boys either in body or in spirit.

Viable Recreational Activities for Love-Shys

The following activities are appropriate for Coed Scouts. However, I also strongly recommend that elementary school and junior high school administrators give serious consideration to offering these activities as physical education alternatives to boys who are fearful, socially withdrawn, and who run away from competitive sports. It is far better for a shy, socially withdrawn boy to be involved in some recreational activities than in none at all. Most importantly, it is definitely better that a behaviorally-inhibited child be allowed to cultivate some friends than no friends at all. Forcing square pegs into round holes is always counterproductive.

1. Bowling
2. Ping Pong (Table Tennis)
3. Miniature Golf
4. Golf
5. Volleyball
6. Lawn Bowling (highly popular in Australia, New Zealand, and England)
7. Boccie (an Italian variety of lawn bowling played on a small court)
8. Horseshoes
9. Billiards (pool)
10. Darts
11. Archery
12. Croquet (another gentle sport that is popular throughout the United Kingdom)
13. Shuffle Board
14. Frisbee Throwing
15. Frisbee Throwing with Dogs
16. Horseback Riding
17. Swimming
18. Bicycle Riding
19. Hiking
20. Musical Theatre productions
21. Stage Plays
22. Ballroom and Social Dancing
23. Square Dancing
24. Hopscotch
25. Tetherball
26. Jump Rope

27. Racquetball
28. Tennis
29. Dog Training and Grooming Activities
30. Arts and Crafts (including sculpting, working with clay, painting, woodwork, etc.)

Physical Education Alternatives

We must discourage the shyness-generating situations to which our male children are exposed throughout their formative years. I believe this can be accomplished without imposing strain on tight school budgets and without inconveniencing boys who truly prefer traditional games. All children should be expected to take part in some sports activities. But all children must be accorded a choice. The available choices for children of all age levels must be made sufficiently varied to accommodate those of the behaviorally-inhibited native temperament. School districts are already required by law to accommodate the blind, the deaf, and children of all intelligence levels who are slow in learning how to read. Similar accommodations must also be made for children who are socially exceptional. Just as slow readers are given a set of learning experiences different from that of the majority of children, a different set of classroom experiences must be developed for shy, socially handicapped children.

Towards this end I believe that a recreation and physical education program that is in harmony with the psychoemotional needs of all children constitutes one of the most promising means for the prevention of chronic and intractable love-shyness. Such a program of recreation and physical education must incorporate three basic ingredients: (1) children must be permitted a choice of activities other than strenuous sports and games; (2) coeducational sports and games must always be available for those children who want them; and (3) behaviorally-inhibited boys must never be required to play with bullies or tough little boys who like to roughhouse.

This third point is of special importance. For even if the game is tiddleywinks, if an inhibited boy is assigned to play alongside a rough boy, the inhibited boy will very soon be bullied and he will withdraw.

While the assertive, aggressive boys happily pursue their football, basketball, and baseball, the more withdrawn boys must have the right to pursue their volleyball, bowling, miniature golf and swimming, etc. And they must have a right to enjoy these activities in a coeducational setting.

Again, socially withdrawn boys typically feel out of place in all-male contexts. When placed in these situations, they fantasize about being with girls anyway. Lacking sisters as many of them do, they desperately need to learn how to interact comfortably with girls and to engage in mutually enjoyable small talk. Hence, it is best that all of their required physical education activities be taken on a strictly coeducational basis. Such a background of coeducation may accord them the head start they need over their more fortunate male peers to feel comfortable about associating informally with girls.

Bullies Must Be Dealt With

Peer bullying is a form of child abuse, and if love-shyness is to be prevented, it must be recognized as such. Peer bullying differs from what is ordinarily thought of as child abuse in that it victimizes male children only and is perpetuated by children themselves rather than by parents and other adult figures. The data presented in this book strongly support the premise that a history of chronic victimization by bullies exists in the childhood backgrounds of a large majority of severely love-shy adults. Thus, bullying causes inhibited boys to fear and to avoid their fellow human beings. It forces inhibited males to grow up as inadequately-socialized isolates. And it is my contention that unless and until all forms of bullying behavior are stopped, chronic and severe love-shyness will continue to plague a significant percentage of America's male adults.

Psychologist Howard Kaplan's work on aggression has revealed that arbitrary and capricious victimization by aggression is much more likely if the victimized individual is perceived by the perpetrator as being either unable and/or unwilling to retaliate. Pre-love-shy elementary school boys develop a reputation very early in life for being both unwilling and unable to defend themselves and fight back. The majority of love-shy men studied for this book had been pacifists (both ideologically and out of fear) throughout their formative years. In a supposedly free society, why shouldn't a male child have a right to be a pacifist and remain free from both physical and psychological harassment and persecution by bullies?

A problematical home life may function to increase the chances that a particular child will gravitate towards finding satisfaction in the hazing and bullying of others. But a problematical home life is never a sufficient cause by itself to assure that a child will bully and harass others. Most male children who come from disturbing or less-than-happy homes do not bully or haze others. Thus, chronic bullies most probably possess an aggressive extrovert native temperament that is catalyzed into action by internalized cultural values and ideals that glorify forms of competition incorporating physical contact.

Psychologist Dan Olweus (University of Bergen) has extensively studied schoolyard bullies in Norway, the United States, and Sweden. The most salient common denominator that he found among bullies is an overriding lack of empathy and compassion. Olweus also found that bullies are quite typically good-looking, above average in intelligence, and highly self-assured. But he also found that their deficits in compassion and empathy render them potentially very dangerous and prone during later adolescence and early adulthood to engage in criminal activity.

I would recommend immediate suspension from school for any and all bullying behavior. Such action should be taken with respect to bullies of all age levels for a minimum of one full day. In addition, Dan Olweus has found behavior modification programs to be highly effective in curbing bullying tendencies. These should be used in addition to one and two-day suspensions.

The Legal Right to Sue

In criminology today there is an increasing and much welcomed trend toward the assuring and protecting of the victim's rights. Even though it may come as a surprise to some readers, children do have the legal right to sue for damages in civil court. And in most jurisdictions they also have the right to sue on assault and battery charges in criminal court. Most children—and parents—are totally unaware of their legal rights, not only with respect to peer bullies, but also with respect to adults (including parents and relatives) who might be guilty of child abuse, neglect, sexual abuse, and/or psychoemotional harassment.

If we are serious about preventing severe love-shyness, we need to occasionally remind children in the classroom setting about how to file complaints with legal, social welfare, and education authorities, against those who might be wronging them. Above all, behaviorally-inhibited children need to be shown in easy-to-understand language how to bring legal charges against those who assault them.

An adult "defends himself" against bullies by consulting with an attorney. *That* is the way defense is supposed to be handled in the United States, *not* by using violence to counteract violence! I believe that free, state-financed attorneys (expert in understanding and in communicating with children) should be made easily available to all children, and especially to those who are behaviorally inhibited.

A Non-Punitive Antidote for Bullying

Anthropologists have documented the fact that bullying among male children is almost unknown in societies that do not glorify competition. With proper safeguards, competition can bring the best out of people, and can assure high quality products and services. In stark contrast, competition involving physical activities almost always invites conflict and wastes human resources. Simply put, competition is far less effective than cooperation at inspiring mutually gratifying interaction and friendly sociability. Indeed, competition (especially in physical activities) is almost always antithetical to effective cooperation and to the ability of people to work together peacefully, harmoniously, and productively.

It is important to note that many persons simply withdraw from competition whenever they lose too regularly.

In singing the praises of competition, many people overlook the important fact that although competition stimulates those who win fairly often, it discourages those who nearly always lose. The slow learner in the classroom, the athletic dub on the playground, *the adolescent who fails to draw the interest of the opposite sex*—such persons usually quit trying, for the pain of repeated failure becomes unendurable. They withdraw from competition in these areas, having decided that the activity isn't worthwhile. There is even experimental evidence that repeated failures not only dampen one's willingness to compete, but may even impair one's actual ability to compete. . . . It appears that repeated failures will fill people with such a sense of incompetence and such an overwhelming expectation of failure that they are unable to use their abilities to good advantage. Success or failure becomes self-perpetuating. There is ample experimental evidence that feelings of self-confidence and expectations of success will improve performance. . . . Even the expectations of other people have been found to affect one's ability to perform well. . . . Repeated failures destroy both the willingness and the ability to compete. (Horton, Paul B., and Chester L. Hunt, *Sociology*, 4th Edition, 1976, p. 296.)

Sociologist Urie Bronfenbrenner has done research on the Soviet system of education. In his studies of a large number of elementary schools in the Ukraine, he observed children engaged in spontaneous play and noticed that there was never any bullying or rough horseplay of the sort which is so commonplace here in the United States. He further learned that any sort of peer bullying is very much against Russian norms.

Russian schools foster an interesting social arrangement from which we here in America could stand to learn a very great deal. Beginning with the fourth grade, every nine-year-old child is assigned to another child of his/her own gender, who is three years younger than he/she is. Thus, every child from the fourth grade through the twelfth grade is assigned to and is responsible for a charge. If that charge falls behind in his/her schoolwork, the elder child is viewed as responsible, and that elder child (along with his/

her entire classroom) loses valued points. Similarly, if someone's younger child is mistreated or teased, it is considered the hard, fast responsibility of the child three years his senior to stop the teasing and to do the necessary protecting.

Most Russian children spend a great deal of their after-school playtime with the child three years younger than themselves to whom they had been assigned. They instruct and tutor him/her in both academic and social skills. Along with obviating the sort of bullying and hazing which prevails in almost all elementary schools in the Untied States, Bronfenbrenner asserts that this pairing up of older child with younger child teaches a great deal about social responsibility, empathy and compassion.

As Bronfenbrenner's work made clear, there is competition in the Soviet Union. But it is invariably a matter of groups of people competing against groups of people, rather than having individuals compete against individuals, as we do here in the United States. The advantage of group-based competition is that children learn early in life to care about the propitious growth and development of other people besides just themselves. In a painless and often enjoyable way, they learn to want to help each other instead of bullying and harassing individuals who are less competitive or seemingly less competent than themselves. Simply put, Russian children are taught to care about their age-mates, and especially about their "charge" three years younger than they, to whom each Soviet child is assigned and for whom they are responsible.

It seems to me that peer group avoidance and quite possibly love-shyness itself could be almost totally prevented through the adopting of a plan similar to the foregoing. Indeed, such a plan could be extended to include all people in society up to the age of 25. Hence, each 25-year-old would be assigned to a college or university senior; and each university senior would be assigned to a university freshman; and each university freshman would be assigned to a high school sophomore, etc. With this sort of benign regimen, cases of incipient long-term love-shyness could be nipped in the bud. Every young man and woman in college and in high school would have ample opportunities for dating members of the opposite sex because every high school and college student's "big brother" or "big sister" would see to it that he/she did—and that he/she was actively involved in gaining the necessary social self-confidence and interpersonal finesse vis-a-vis the opposite sex for effective adjustment throughout adult life.

Lest the reader suspect that this sort of regimen might undermine academic mastery, it should be stated in no uncertain terms that Russian students at all education levels tend to be much more serious and much more accomplished than their American counterparts. For example, chronic cases of underachievement and truancy are very seldom seen in the Soviet Union.

In sum, bullying and hazing, and quite possibly love-shyness itself, can be prevented through assigning every child to a "big brother" or "big sister" three years his/her senior. Besides enabling children to achieve better grades in school, such a procedure could well eliminate pathological shyness through helping children in an enjoyable and benign way to develop strong interpersonal skills and social self-confidence.

High School Practice-Dating Programs

Practice-dating therapy can be expected to work both faster and easier for high school teenagers than for university young people. Practice-dating programs at the high school level constitute strong preventive medicine that will ultimately benefit not only the treated love-shy individuals, but the wider society as well.

In terms of organization, I would recommend that sets of three or four area high schools group-up with each other. This way each "set" could manage an especially well-run practice-dating program that would provide all shy students with a warmly caring and deeply meaningful support group of close friends of both sexes.

"Shys Anonymous" and "Love-Shys Anonymous" Groups

As I have stressed throughout this book, love-shys do not have any support groups. A key remedy for this deficit would certainly be the creation of nationwide networks of both "Coed Scouts" and "Practice-Dating Therapy" groups. But there is a third type of group which I believe would help. This third organization could be called "Shys Anonymous" or "Love-Shys Anonymous."

Patterned after the Alcoholics Anonymous model, Shys Anonymous would be composed of shy persons of both sexes and of all ages. Through a host of organizational activities significant help, together with positive motivation, would be provided for its membership. The services of professional counselors could also be retained from time to time for purposes of facilitating group interaction, psychodrama, therapeutic role playing, etc. But as is the case with "AA," most meetings would be conducted without the presence of any professional counselor-facilitators.

Shys Anonymous would provide important reinforcement for the adopting of positive behavior and dress patterns. Its membership would display genuine caring and concern for each other, something which most love-shys never experience throughout their formative years, from either parents or peers. Just as homosexual organizations provide true and meaningful friendships for their members, Shys Anonymous would provide an important source of caring friends to the heterosexual love-shy.

Alcoholics, gamblers, drug addicts, child abusers, over-eaters, homosexuals, parents of terminally ill children, parents of gay and lesbian children all have support groups. Severe shyness is one of the very few human problems for which there is no existent support group. The fact that severely shy people are not "joiners" is doubtless a major reason for this. But as I have already stressed, when it comes to shy people, values, attitudes and desires very often do not coincide with overt behaviors. It would be a mistake to infer that love-shys wouldn't want to join a caring support group which might enable them to meet and date an attractive pool of potential marriage partners. Shys Anonymous organizations could also serve as a constructive social-political force; as a kind of lobby group striving toward constructive reforms in the education system and in the family.

Dr. E. Michael Gutman, a psychiatrist and neurologist practicing in Orlando, Florida, has suggested that the following might be used as an organizational statement for Shys Anonymous. He and I hope to launch such an organization within the next five years, with chapters in North America, western Europe, Australia and

New Zealand. Anyone who might be interested in organizing a local chapter of Shys Anonymous or in serving on the Board of Directors should contact either Dr. Gutman or myself.

SHYS ANONYMOUS PREAMBLE

We, the Shy People of the western world, band together for the purpose of tying a common knot that will enable us to congregate, communicate and co-relate with other Shys who have difficulty in breaking the bondage created by the shyness handicap.

We hope:

1. Shys Anonymous will help us to establish friendships.
2. Shys Anonymous will help us with our slavery to behavioral inertia.
3. Shys Anonymous will help us abandon our negativism and pessimism.
4. Shys Anonymous will stop our need to exercise destructive control.
5. Shys Anonymous will keep us from feeling alone, even when we are with relatives and the few friends we have.
6. Shys Anonymous will break our self-consciousness.
7. Shys Anonymous will allow us to achieve sexual intimacy.
8. Shys Anonymous will help us to better relate vis-a-vis the opposite sex.
9. Shys Anonymous will break our inhibition of action and initiating of activity.
10. Shys Anonymous will break paralysis that stymies us in maintaining productivity and efficiency.
11. Shys Anonymous will help us to greatly improve our levels of self-esteem.
12. Shys Anonymous will help us to break the image of seeming to be cold, aloof, distant and selfish.
13. Shys Anonymous will break the pathological streak that allows us to often develop vices and bad habits that take over our lives as a result of our effort to achieve relief from the pain of life.
14. Shys Anonymous will help us to stop being afraid of rejection.
15. Shys Anonymous will be a self-help, political advocacy, and consumer group that will give us a banner to wave and an anchor on which to hold.
16. Shys Anonymous will relieve us of our quirky ways.

Our organization is intended for all shy people from 9 to 90, irrespective of sex, race, creed, religion, ethnicity, physical handicap, or political orientation.

Changing the Norms

One of the most obvious ways of preventing the development of severe love-shyness is to change social norms. After all, if love-shyness is indeed primarily due to a poorness of fit between social expectations and inborn temperament, then it stands to reason that love-shyness will rapidly diminish to the extent that the norms are restructured to be in greater harmony with man's nature.

The major norm in need of changing is the one which stipulates that the male, *not the female* must *always* be the one to make the first move in initiating cross-sexed friendships and informal conversations. I would suggest that native temperament and *not gender* should be the prime determinant in any given situation as to which sex should make the first move towards the initiation of a friendship. There is no evidence that the native temperaments of males and females differ substantially regarding the natural proclivity to be assertive. Women who are naturally assertive should be both permitted and encouraged to make the first move. And, men who are naturally passive should be allowed and encouraged to play the passive role without any cost to them in social respect, honor, esteem, or intimate female companionship. No one should be penalized for attributes that accrue from inborn temperament.

Accordingly, we must stop socializing our little girls into believing that they should never ask boys for dates. Elementary school children at all levels should be exposed to learning experiences which make it very clear that gender should never have anything whatsoever to do with the issue of who should assume the socially assertive role in any given cross-sexed situation. Parents need to be helped towards an understanding as to why the traditional norm prescribing social assertiveness for males but proscribing it for females is destructive and highly deleterious to mental health. They should be helped to understand why this norm needs to be thrown away forever into the trash can and replaced with a normative system that is compassionate and congruent with the needs and natures of human beings.

Inasmuch as the family is the prime socializer of all children, it is quite clear that adults must be won over as to the belief and conviction that certain traditional norms promote love-shyness, loneliness, and poor mental health. Lectures and discussions at PTA meetings might well be a good place at which to commence this effort.

In Hamburg, Berlin, Frankfurt, Munich, and several other German cities, there are some very popular establishments at which women (*only the women*) ask the men for dances. And if a man refuses a given woman he is asked to leave. So far as I am aware, there has never been an establishment anywhere where a *woman* is asked to leave if *she* refuses a man's request for a dance!

Some Final Thoughts

The importance of preventive efforts needs to be underscored with respect to the problem of love-shyness. Whereas it is true that the underlying basis for love-shyness is inborn, the problem itself is learned. Because society reacts, sometimes harshly, to little boys who are inhibited and anxious, the boys tend to develop painful "people-phobias" along with very low self-esteem. When such boys are required to grow up without sisters, they may develop severe and intractable love-shyness. This is especially true when the parents don't know how to manage, understand and accept highly inhibited boys and are isolated from meaningful kin networks.

With respect to the first point, a child cannot change unless he is accepted and respected as he is—highly inhibited or otherwise. Focusing on weaknesses serves to block communication and meaningful growth, whereas concentrating on the strengths of a child tends to open up meaningful communication and encourages participation and positive change. Further, concentrating upon weaknesses tends to strengthen and enhance those very weaknesses.

A key conclusion of child psychiatrist Alexander Thomas has a strong bearing on the development of severe shyness: Behavior disorders, including intractable shyness, are caused by a bad fit between a child's inborn temperament and parental, teacher and peer expectations. As Thomas and others have demonstrated, being born high on behavioral inhibition and nervousness is never enough by itself to create a people-phobia. Thus when an introvert with a low-anxiety threshold is accorded a plentiful abundance of pleasurable play experiences with peers and genuine acceptance from his parents, he *invariably* develops a healthy self-esteem and social self-confidence. As an introvert, he ordinarily prefers just a few very close friends in lieu of having many less close ones; and he will usually prefer play and recreation that is less competitive and more or less on the quiet side. But he will (and this is the important point) be normally sociable. He will be able to enjoy the companionship of others. Hence, my position is that people entering the world with high behavioral inhibition and low anxiety thresholds are not entering the world "sick." I believe that they are made "sick" by a sick society. And it is high time that we started to think seriously about ways of constructively changing this sick society instead of trying all the time to force the individual with difficulties to do all the changing. A person with high inhibition and low anxiety threshold genes can, under propitious circumstances, become fully healthy from a psychoemotional and social behavior standpoint. Females with this combination of genetic characteristics *usually* develop reasonably healthy levels of self-esteem and social self-confidence; and they almost always manage to date and to marry at normally early ages. The only reason why males with these characteristics do not develop strong self-esteem and social self-confidence is that society disapproves of such males and tries to change them. In girls, similar characteristics are usually accepted and respected.

Our society tends to be more understanding and helpful towards maladaptive behavior that is not associated with psychoemotional states of mind. Thus, children with physical or learning disabilities are accorded all manner of special attention. Even slow readers are given special classes along with quite a bit of one-on-one attention to help remedy their problems. We don't tell slow readers: "If we put you in a special class we would be doing you a disservice. This is a competitive world, and the only way you're going to be able to cope with it as an adult is to learn how to cope with it now." Instead we realize that it is only through special training and special attention to specific learning problems that a child will eventually be able to catch up.

This same logic should apply to the inhibited boy. We need to appreciate the fact that being born inhibited and slow to warm up to people socially is analogous to being born with a minor learning disability. We shouldn't bully and disparage shy and inhibited boys. The inhibited boy similarly requires special attention. He requires a coeducational learning environment that is gentle, accepting, non-threatening and non-competitive. If and when he is accorded this he will stand a reasonable chance of one day being able to compete effectively within the mainstream of society.

It is almost axiomatic in our society that people are to be judged by their actions. But you cannot assume that an introvert does not want something simply because he is never observed doing it! Love-shy males are not disinterested in informal boy-girl inter-action. As this book demonstrates, love-shy males become interested in girls substantially earlier in life than non-shy boys do. But unlike the non-shy, love-shy boys spend much of their time and psychoemotional energies at school and at home in a world of wish-fulfillment fantasies and daydreams. This tends to be as true for five-year-old love-shys as it is for those in their 20s and 30s.

Parents, teachers and relatives often think that they are doing a favor for the inhibited boy (who only "*appears*" to be "disinter-ested" in girls) by saying things like "Oh, leave him alone; he's still got plenty of time!" In point of fact, such well-meaning adults are doing a very grave disservice as a result of their laissez-faire posture.

Unless a child presents clear and irrefutable evidence that he is not interested in the opposite sex, ways need to be engineered that effectively facilitate relaxed, comfortable boy-girl interaction. And towards this end I strongly recommend making practice-dating clinics available to all children 15 years of age and older. Inhibited boys of younger ages should be tactfully introduced to the non-threatening activities of Coed Scouting and/or of Shys Anonymous.

One point is certain: Love-shys do not have plenty of time. Love-shy males become increasingly worse off as time passes, never better! A boy who is love-shy at 15 will become more severely and intractably love-shy by the time he reaches 30—unless someone intervenes.

Decisive action must be taken to involve love-shy males in informal activities with girls, and to keep them involved. There must never be any let up in this regard. The love-shy boy must not be left alone until he has finally arrived at the point where he can actually assert himself with women and participate fully in the social life of his community.

Appendix 1

The Survey of Heterosexual Interactions ("SHI Questionnaire")

This scale was employed for determining eligibility for inclusion in the *non-shy* sample. It has the benefit of national statistical norms, and it has been used in many different research studies. It was originally designed by psychologists Craig T. Twentyman and Richard M. McFall of the University of Wisconsin at Madison.

> *INSTRUCTIONS:* Please circle the appropriate number in the following situations. Try to respond as if you were actually in that situation.

1. You want to call a girl up for a date. This is the first time you are calling her up as you only know her slightly. When you get ready to make the call, your roommate comes into the room, sits down on his bed, and begins reading a magazine. In this situation you would:

1	2	3	4	5	6	7
be unable to call in every case		be able to call in some cases			be able to call in every case	

2. You are at a dance. You see a very attractive girl whom you do not know. She is standing *alone* and you would like to dance with her. You would:

1	2	3	4	5	6	7
be unable to ask her in every case		be able to ask her in some cases			be able to ask her in every case	

3. You are at a party and you see two girls talking. You do not know these girls but you would like to know one of them better. In this situation you would:

1	2	3	4	5	6	7
be unable to initiate a conversation		be able to initiate a conversation in some cases			be able to initiate a conversation in every case	

4. You are at a bar where there is also dancing. You see a couple of girls sitting in a booth. One, whom you do not know, is talking with a fellow who is standing by the booth. These two go over to dance leaving the other girl sitting alone. You have seen this girl around, but do not really know her. You would like to go over and talk to her (but you wouldn't like to dance). In this situation you would:

1	2	3	4	5	6	7
be unable to go over and talk to her		be able to go over and talk to her in some cases			be able to go over and talk to her in every case	

5. On a work break at your job you see a girl who also works there and is about your age. You would like to talk to her, but you do not know her. You would:

1	2	3	4	5	6	7
be unable to talk to her in every case		be able to talk to her in some cases			be able to talk to her in every case	

6. You are on a crowded bus. A girl you know *only slightly* is sitting in front of you. You would like to talk to her but you

notice that the fellow sitting next to her is watching you. You would:

1	2	3	4	5	6	7

be unable to talk to her in every case   be able to talk to her in some cases   be able to talk to her in every case.

7. You are at a dance. You see an attractive girl whom you do not know, standing *in a group* of four girls. You would like to dance. In this situation you would:

1	2	3	4	5	6	7

be unable to ask in every case   be able to ask in some cases   be able to ask in every case

8. You are at a drugstore counter eating lunch. A girl whom you do not know sits down beside you. You would like to talk to her. After her meal comes she asks you to pass the sugar. In this situation you would pass the sugar:

1	2	3	4	5	6	7

but be unable to initiate a conversation with her   and in some cases be able to initiate a conversation   and be able to initiate a conversation

9. A friend of yours is going out with his girlfriend this weekend. He wants you to come along and gives you the name and phone number of a girl he says would be a good date. You are not doing anything this weekend. In this situation you would:

1	2	3	4	5	6	7

be unable to call in every case   be able to call her in some cases   be able to call in every case

10. You are at the library. You decide to take a break, and as you walk down the hall you see a girl whom you know only casually. She is sitting at a table and appears to be studying. You decide that you would like to ask her to get a Coke with you. In this situation you would:

1	2	3	4	5	6	7

be unable to ask her in every case	be able to ask her in some cases	be able to ask her in every case

11. You want to call a girl up for a date. You find this girl attractive but you do not know her. You would:

1	2	3	4	5	6	7

be unable to call in every case	be able to call in some cases	be able to call in every case

12. You are taking a class at the university. After one of your classes you see a girl whom you know. You would like to talk to her; however, she is walking with a couple of other girls you do not know. You would:

1	2	3	4	5	6	7

be unable to talk to her in every case	be able to talk to her in some cases	be able to talk to her in every case

13. You have been working on a committee for the past year. There is a banquet at which you are assigned a particular seat. On one side of you there is a girl you do not know; on the other side is a guy you do not know. In this situation you would:

1	2	3	4	5	6	7

be unable to initiate a conversation with the girl and talk only with the guy	be able to initiate a conversation with the girl in some cases but talk mostly to the guy	be able to initiate a conversation in every case and be able to talk equally as freely with the girl as with the guy

14. You are in the lobby of a large apartment complex waiting for a friend. As you are waiting for him to come down, a girl whom you know well walks by with another girl whom you have never seen before. The girl you know says hello and begins to talk to you. Suddenly she remembers that she left something in her room. Just before she leaves you she tells you the other girl's name. In this situation you would:

1	2	3	4	5	6	7

find it very
difficult to
initiate and
continue a
conversation with
the other girl

find it only slightly
difficult

find it easy to
initiate and
continue a
conversation

15. You are at a party in a friend's apartment. You see a girl who
has come alone. You don't know her, but you would like to
talk to her. In this situation you would:

1	2	3	4	5	6	7

be unable to go
over and talk to
her

be able to go over and
talk to her in some cases

be able to go
over and talk to
her in every case

16. You are walking to your mailbox in the large apartment building where you live. When you get there you notice that two
girls are putting their names on the mailbox of the vacant
apartment beneath yours. In this situation you would:

1	2	3	4	5	6	7

be unable to go
over and initiate a
conversation

be able to go over and
initiate a conversation in
some cases

be able to go
over and initiate
a conversation in
every case

17. You are at a record store and see a girl that you once were
introduced to. That was several months ago and now you have
forgotten her name. You would like to talk to her. In this
situation you would:

1	2	3	4	5	6	7

be unable to start
a conversation
with her in every
case

be able to start a
conversation with her in
some cases

be able to start a
conversation
with her in every
case

18. You are at the student union or local cafeteria where friends of
your age eat lunch. You have gotten your meal and are now

looking for a place to sit down. Unfortunately, there are no empty tables. At one table, however, there is a girl sitting alone. In this situation you would:

1	2	3	4	5	6	7
wait until another place was empty and then sit down		ask the girl if you could sit at the table but not say anything more to her			ask the girl if you could sit at the table and then initiate a conversation	

19. A couple of weeks ago you had a first-date with a girl you now see walking on the street towards you. For some reason you haven't seen each other since then. You would like to talk to her but aren't sure of what she thinks of you. In this situation you would:

1	2	3	4	5	6	7
walk by without saying anything		walk up to her and say something in some cases			walk up to her and say something in every case	

20. Generally, in most social situations involving girls whom I do not know, I would:

1	2	3	4	5	6	7
be unable to initiate a conversation		be able to initiate a conversation in some cases			be able to initiate a conversation in every case	

SCORING: The foregoing twenty items comprise the "SHI Questionnaire." It is scored by simply adding up the circled numbers for each one of the twenty items. Scores can range from a low of 20 to a high of 140. The *lower* a man's score, the more *love-shy* he is likely to be.

Appendix 2

The Gilmartin Love-Shyness Scale

This scale is included here for the benefit of researchers who might want to use it in their own work. The numbers which are indicated underneath each item are for purposes of *coding*. The *higher* a man's score, the more severely love-shy he is. The *lower* a person's score is, the more self-confident and *non*-shy he is likely to be in friendly, casual encounters vis-a-vis the opposite sex. Whereas the scale ("GLSS") was intended for males only, it can be used for women if the items containing an asterisk (*) are first removed.

1. I feel relaxed even in unfamiliar social situations.
   0 True;   1 False.
2. I try to avoid situations which force me to be very sociable.
   1 True;   0 False.
3. It is easy for me to relax when I am with strangers.
   0 True;   1 False.
4. I have no particular desire to avoid people.
   0 True;   1 False
5. I often find social situations upsetting.
   1 True;   0 False

6. I usually feel calm and comfortable at social occasions.
   0 True;   1 False
7. I am usually at ease when talking to someone of the opposite sex
   0 True;   1 False
8. I try to avoid talking to people unless I know them well.
   1 True;   0 False.
9. If the chance comes to meet new people, I often take it.
   0 True;   1 False.
10. I often feel nervous or tense in casual get-togethers in which both sexes are present.
    1 True;   0 False
11. I am usually nervous with people unless I know them well.
    1 True;   0 False.
12. I usually feel relaxed when I am with a group of people.
    0 True;   1 False
13. I often want to get away from people.
    1 True;   0 False.
14. I usually feel uncomfortable when I am in a group of people I don't know.
    1 True;   0 False.
15. I usually feel relaxed when I meet someone for the first time.
    0 True;   1 False.
16. Being introduced to people makes me tense and nervous.
    1 True;   0 False.
17. I find it very difficult to display emotion and feeling.
    1 True;   0 False.
18. I would avoid walking up and joining a large group of people.
    1 True;   0 False.
19. After I was about 13 or so I usually tried not to sing out loud whenever anyone was around.
    1 True;   0 False.
20. I tend to withdraw from people.
    1 True;   0 False.

21. I often feel on edge when I am with a group of people.
1 True;   0 False.

22. I find it easy to start conversations with people of the opposite sex in informal social situations.
0 True;   1 False.

23. I sometimes take the responsibility for introducing people to each other.
0 True;   1 False.

24. When I like someone I am able to let them know it without difficulty.
0 True;   1 False.

25. I find it easy to relax with other people.
0 True;   1 False.

26. I often feel that I don't know what to say in certain types of informal social situations.
1 True;   0 False.

27. When I would like to be friendly with someone, I often feel that I know what to say but I just haven't got the nerve to say it.
1 True;   0 False.

28. It requires a tremendous amount of nerve to be friendly with the opposite sex.
4 Strongly agree.
3 Agree.
2 Uncertain.
1 Disagree.
0 Strongly disagree.

*29. I am proficient at making friendly overtures to the opposite sex.
0 Very true of me.
1 On the most part true of me.
2 Slightly true of me.
3 Not true of me.
4 Very untrue of me.

30. It wouldn't bother me at all if I had no friends of my own sex. Just so long as I had friends of the opposite sex I'd be alright.
4 Strongly agree.

3 Agree.

2 Uncertain.

1 Disagree.

0 Strongly disagree.

31. The idea of starting a conversation with someone of the opposite sex whom I do not know and in whom I have a secret romantic interest is very frightening to me.

2 True;   0 False.

32. How optimistic are you that you will be able to overcome a sufficient amount of your shyness to enable you to find a partner and get married?

0 I am *NOT* shy.

1 Very optimistic.

2 Somewhat optimistic.

3 Slightly optimistic.

4 Not optimistic.

33. I am sure that it would do me a very great deal of good if I had one or two really close friends who would (figuratively speaking) take me by the hand and help me get involved with the opposite sex.

4 Strongly agree.

3 Agree.

2 Uncertain.

1 Disagree.

0 Strongly disagree.

*34. How confident are you right now about *initiating* love-making (not necessarily sexual) with someone of the opposite sex with whom you would like to make love?

0 Very confident.

1 Confident.

2 Fairly confident.

3 Not too confident.

4 Lacking in confidence.

35. I have hesitated to make or to accept dates because of shyness.

2 True;   0 False

*36. Do you envy women for the passive role they are permitted to play in dating and courtship?

3 Frequently.
2 Sometimes.
1 Rarely.
0 Never.

*37. I would like to see arranged marriages available as an option in our society so that I could get married without having to suffer the indignity of having to ask women for dates.
2 True;   0 False.

38. How satisfied are you with your current dating frequency?
5 Very dissatisfied.
4 Dissatisfied.
3 Slightly dissatisfied.
2 Slightly satisfied.
1 Moderately satisfied.
0 Very satisfied.

39. How satisfied are you with the amount of informal boy/girl interaction you are currently engaging in these days?
5 Very dissatisfied.
4 Dissatisfied.
3 Slightly dissatisfied.
2 Slightly satisfied.
1 Moderately satisfied.
0 Very satisfied.

40. *Before* you were 13 years old, did you ever experience loneliness for the close, emotionally meaningful companionship of an age-mate *of the opposite sex?*
2 Yes;   0 No.

41. I would much rather not date at all than date someone whose face is insufficiently attractive to please my aesthetic and romantic sensibilities.
2 True.
1 Uncertain.
0 False.

42. I would not want to date anyone to whom I could not visualize (fantasize) myself as being married.
2 True.
1 Uncertain.
0 False.

43. I have never made love (not necessarily sexual love) in my life.

   2 True;   0 False.

44. Would you be too shy to ask the clerk in a drug store for a package of condoms or vaginal foam?

   2 Yes;   0 No.

45. There have been times when I have stared for long periods at a person of the opposite sex whom I have found attractive. But as soon as she/he would look in my direction I would immediately look away.

   3 True.

   2 True; but I've only done this once or twice.

   1 False; but I have had the urge to do this.

   0 False.

46. There have been times when I have *followed* a person of the opposite sex whom I have found attractive. But as soon as she/he would look in my direction I would immediately look away.

   3 True.

   2 True; but I've only done this once or twice.

   1 False; but I have had the urge to do this.

   0 False.

47. Sometimes I get the feeling that society does everything in its power to keep the two sexes separated from each other.

   2 True;   0 False.

48. How confident are you at present in associating with the other sex?

   0 Very confident.

   1 Confident.

   2 Fairly confident.

   3 Not too confident.

   4 Lacking in confidence.

*49. When I was a child of about 10 or 11, there was nothing I used to spend more time daydreaming about than little girls of my age or younger.

   2 True;   0 False.

50. I have been in love with a number of people of the opposite sex who were not even aware of my existence.
    1 True; 0 False.

51. On a 10-point scale with "*10*" representing the extremely handsome or beautiful end and "*0*" representing the ugly end, how would you rate your own *current* physical attractiveness?
    Give number:(*Coding*: 0 = *10;* 1 = *9;* 2 = *8;* 3 = *7;* 4 = *6;*
    5 = *5;* 6 = *4;* 7 = *3;* 8 = *2;* 9 = *1;* 10 = *0.*)

52. It requires a tremendous amount of nerve to be friendly with people.
    4 Strongly agree.
    3 Agree.
    2 Uncertain.
    1 Disagree.
    0 Strongly disagree.

53. There is little if anything in life more frightening or overwhelming to me than the thought of experiencing anxiety.
    4 Strongly agree.
    3 Agree.
    2 Uncertain.
    1 Disagree.
    0 Strongly disagree.

54. How often do you worry about having things to talk about with people?
    4 Very frequently.
    3 Frequently.
    2 Sometimes.
    1 Seldom.
    0 Never.

55. I am far less friendly with people than I would really like to be.
    2 True; 0 False.

56. It would overwhelm me with extremely painful feelings of anxiety to accidentally say "hello" to someone on the street who, upon closer examination, turned out to be a

total stranger instead of the person to whom I thought I
had said "hello".

    3 True.

    2 I'd be upset, but it wouldn't unruffle me *that* much.

    1 Uncertain.

    0 False.

57. People often misunderstand, misinterpret, or "misread"
the way I act or fail to act.

    4 Very true.

    3 Somewhat true.

    2 Slightly true.

    1 Not true.

    0 Very untrue.

58. I often feel that I lack free choice and self-determination
because of my shyness.

    4 Very true of me.

    3 Somewhat true of me.

    2 Slightly true of me.

    1 Not true of me.

    0 Very untrue of me.

59. My shyness has caused me to be incorrectly seen by some
people as a homosexual.

    4 Very true of me.

    3 Somewhat true of me.

    2 Slightly true of me.

    1 Not true of me.

    0 Very untrue of me.

60. How severe a problem is shyness for your life at this time?

    4 Very severe.

    3 Somewhat severe.

    2 A moderate problem.

    1 A slight problem.

    0 Not a problem.

NOTE: *This scale assumes that the person taking it is (1) single, never
married; and (2) heterosexual.*

Bibliography

Asher, Jules. 1987.
"Born to be Shy?" PSYCHOLOGY TODAY (April):56-64.

Azrin, Nathan. 1979.
THE PSYCHOLOGY OF JOB HUNTING. New York: Ziff-Davis.

Berscheid, Ellen, and Karen Dion. 1971.
"Physical Attractiveness and Dating Choice: A Test of the Matching Hypothesis." JOURNAL OF EXPERIMENTAL SOCIAL PSYCHOLOGY 7, pp. 173-189.

Berscheid, Ellen and Elaine Walster. 1974.
"Physical Attractiveness." In Berkowitz, L. (Ed.), ADVANCES IN EXPERIMENTAL SOCIAL PSYCHOLOGY (Vol. 7), New York: Academic Press, pp. 157-215.

Bronfenbrenner, Urie. 1970.
TWO WORLDS OF CHILDHOOD: U.S. AND U.S.S.R. New York: Russell Sage Foundation.

Caspi, Avshalom, Glen H. Elder, Jr., & Daryl J. Bem. 1988.
"Moving Away from the World: Life-Course Patterns of Shy Children." DEVELOPMENTAL PSYCHOLOGY 24 (No. 6): 824-831

Cassill, Kay. 1982.
TWINS: NATURE'S AMAZING MYSTERY. New York: Atheneum.

Chess, Stella, and Alexander Thomas. 1987.
KNOW YOUR CHILD. New York: Basic Books.

Cousins, Norman. 1984.
MIND OVER ILLNESS. Chicago: Nightengale-Conant.

Daniels, Denise, and Robert Plomin. 1985.
"Shy Baby Genes." PSYCHOLOGY TODAY *19* (June): 16-17.

Dorner, Gunter. 1980.
"Sexual Differentiation of the Brain." VITAMINS AND HOR-
MONES *38*, pp. 235-280.

Dorner, Gunter, 1981.
"Sex Hormones and Neurotransmitters as Mediators for Sexual Differentiation of the Brain." ENDOKRINOLOGIE *78*, pp. 586-650.

Durden-Smith, Jo, and Diane DeSimone. 1983.
SEX AND THE BRAIN. New York: Arbor House.

Dworkin, Robert H., et. al. 1976.
"A Longitudinal Study of the Genetics of Personality." JOURNAL
OF PERSONALITY AND SOCIAL PSYCHOLOGY *34*, pp. 510-
518.

Dyer, Wayne. 1985.
WHAT DO YOU *REALLY* WANT FOR YOUR CHILDREN? New
York: William Morrow.

Ehrhardt, Anke A., and Heine F. Meyer-Bahlburg. 1981.
"Effects of Prenatal Sex Hormones on Gender-Related Behavior."
SCIENCE. March 20.

Ellis, Robert A., and W. Clayton Lane. 1967.
"Social Mobility and Social Isolation." AMERICAN SOCIOLOGI-
CAL REVIEW *32* (June): 237-256.

Eysenck, Hans J. 1967.
THE BIOLOGICAL BASIS OF PERSONALITY. Springfield, Illinois: Charles C. Thomas.

Eysenck, Hans J. 1976.
"Genetic Factors in Personality Development." In Kaplan, A.R.
(Ed.), HUMAN BEHAVIOR GENETICS. Springfield, Illinois:
Charles C. Thomas, pp. 198-229.

Eysenck, Hans J. 1976.
SEX AND PERSONALITY. Austin: University of Texas Press.

Freedman, Jonathan, and Anthony N. Doob. 1968.
DEVIANCY: THE PSYCHOLOGY OF BEING DIFFERENT. New
York: Academic Press.

Freedman, Jonathan. 1978.
HAPPY PEOPLE: WHAT HAPPINESS IS, WHO HAS IT, AND WHY. New York: Harcourt Brace Jovanovich.

Fromm, Erich. 1956.
THE ART OF LOVING. New York: Harper & Row.

Garcia-Coll, Cynthia. 1981.
"Psychophysiological Correlates of a Tendency Toward Inhibition in Infants." Unpublished Doctoral Dissertation. Cambridge: Harvard University.

Garcia-Coll, Cynthia, and Jerome Kagan. 1984.
"Behavioral Inhibition to the Unfamiliar." CHILD DEVELOPMENT 55 (December): 2212-2225.

Gilmartin, Brian G. 1965.
"Relationship of Traits Measured by the California Psychological Inventory to Premarital Sexual Standards and Behaviors." Unpublished Masters Thesis. Salt Lake City: University of Utah.

Gilmartin, Brian. 1979.
"Corporal Punishment: A Research Update." HUMAN BEHAVIOR 8 (February): 18-25.

Gilmartin, Brian G. 1985.
"Some Family Antecedents of Severe Shyness in Males." FAMILY RELATIONS 34 (July): 429-438

Gilmartin, Brian G. 1987.
"Peer Group Antecedents of Severe Love-Shyness in Males." JOURNAL OF PERSONALITY 55 (September): 467-489.

Gilmartin, Brian G. 1987.
SHYNESS AND LOVE: CAUSES, CONSEQUENCES AND TREATMENT. Lanham, Maryland: University Press of America.

Ginzberg, Eli. 1969.
MEN, MONEY AND MEDICINE. New York: Columbia University Press.

Gordon, Thomas. 1970.
PARENT EFFECTIVENESS TRAINING. New York: Wyden Books.

Gordon, Thomas. 1976.
P.E.T. IN ACTION. New York: Wyden Books.

Gottesman, Irving I. 1966.
"Genetic Variance in Adaptive Personality Traits." JOURNAL OF CHILD PSYCHOLOGY AND PSYCHIATRY 7, pp. 199-208.

Goy, Robert, and Bruce McEwen. 1980.
SEXUAL DIFFERENTIATION OF THE BRAIN. Cambridge: M.I.T. Press.

Grant, Vernon W. 1976.
FALLING IN LOVE: THE PSYCHOLOGY OF THE ROMANTIC EMOTION. New York: Springer.

Gutman, E. Michael. 1982.
"The Shyness Disorder: Should it be Included in the DSM-IV?" Paper Presented at the Annual Meeting of the Florida Psychiatric Society, Tampa, Florida, November 20.

Gutman, E. Michael. 1980.
WHAT'S WRONG WITH ME, DOC? Tampa, Florida: Cody Publishers.

Harlow, Harry F., and Margaret K. Harlow. 1962.
"Social Deprivation in Monkeys." SCIENTIFIC AMERICAN 207 (November): 136-146.

Hill, Charles T., Letitia Anne Peplau, and Zick Rubin. 1976.
"Breakups Before Marriage: The End of 103 Affairs." JOURNAL OF SOCIAL ISSUES 32 (No. 1): 147-168.

Horton, Paul B., and Chester L. Hunt. 1976.
SOCIOLOGY (4th edition), New York: McGraw-Hill.

Jencks, Christopher, et. al. 1977.
WHO GETS AHEAD? THE DETERMINANTS OF ECONOMIC SUCCESS IN AMERICA. New York: Basic Books.

Johnson, Spencer. 1983.
THE ONE MINUTE FATHER. New York: William Morrow & Company.

Johnson, Spencer. 1983.
THE ONE MINUTE MOTHER. New York: William Morrow & Company.

Jones, Warren H., Jonathan M. Cheek, and Stephen R. Briggs (Eds.), SHYNESS: PERSPECTIVES ON RESEARCH AND TREATMENT. New York: Plenum Press, 1986.

Kagan, Jerome. 1982
"The Fearful Child's Hidden Talents." PSYCHOLOGY TODAY 16 (July): 50-59.

Kagan, Jerome, and Howard A. Moss. 1983.
BIRTH TO MATURITY. New Haven: Yale University Press.

Kagan, Jerome. 1984.
"Behavioral Inhibition in the Young Child." CHILD DEVELOPMENT 55 (June): 1005-1014.

Kagan, Jerome, & J. Steven Reznick. 1988.
"Biological Bases of Childhood Shyness." SCIENCE *240* (April): 167-171.

Kaplan, Howard B. 1980.
DEVIANT BEHAVIOR IN DEFENSE OF SELF. New York: Academic Press.

Kersey, Katherine C. 1986.
THE NEUROPSYCHOLOGY OF SUCCESSFUL PARENTING. Newark, California: SyberVision.

Klein, Donald F., and Judith G. Rabkin. 1981.
ANXIETY: NEW RESEARCH AND CHANGING CONCEPTS. New York: Raven Press.

Knox, David, and Kenneth Wilson. 1981.
"Dating Behaviors of University Students." FAMILY RELATIONS *30* (April): 255-258.

Knox, David, and Kenneth Wilson. 1983.
"Dating Problems of University Students." COLLEGE STUDENT JOURNAL *17*, pp. 225-228.

Knupfer, Genevieve, et. al. 1966.
"The Mental Health of the Unmarried." AMERICAN JOURNAL OF PSYCHIATRY *122*, pp. 841–851.

Komarovsky, Mirra. 1976.
DILEMMAS OF MASCULINITY: A STUDY OF COLLEGE YOUTH. New York: Norton.

Landis, Judson T., and Mary G. Landis. 1973.
BUILDING A SUCCESSFUL MARRIAGE. Englewood Cliffs, New Jersey: Prentice-Hall.

Lazarus, Arnold. 1977.
IN THE MIND'S EYE. New York: Rawson.

Liebowitz, Michael R. 1983.
THE CHEMISTRY OF LOVE. Boston: Little, Brown.

MacLaine, Shirley. 1985.
DANCING IN THE LIGHT. New York: Basic Books.

Montagu, Ashley. 1971.
TOUCHING: THE HUMAN SIGNIFICANCE OF THE SKIN. New York: Harper and Row.

Moss, Thelma. 1979.
THE BODY ELECTRIC. Los Angeles: J. P. Tarcher, Inc.

Olweus, Dan. 1977.
"Aggression and Peer Acceptance in Adolescent Boys." CHILD
DEVELOPMENT 48, pp. 978-987.

Olweus, Dan. 1978.
AGGRESSION IN THE SCHOOLS: BULLIES AND WHIPPING
BOYS. Washington, D. C.: Hemisphere.

Olweus,Dan. 1984.
"Aggressors and their Victims: Bullying at School." In Frude, Neil,
and Hugh Gault (Eds.), DISRUPTIVE BEHAVIOR IN SCHOOLS.
New York: John Wiley.

Peplau, Letitia Anne. 1979.
UNDERSTANDING AND OVERCOMING LONELINESS. New
York: Ziff-Davis.

Peplau, Letitia Anne, and Daniel Perlman. 1982.
LONELINESS: A SOURCEBOOK OF CURRENT THEORY,
RESEARCH AND THERAPY. New York: John Wiley.

Pilkonis, Paul A. 1977.
"Shyness, Public and Private, and its Relationship to Other Measures
of Social Behavior." JOURNAL OF PERSONALITY 45 (No. 4):
585-595.

Pilkonis, Paul A. 1977.
"The Behavioral Consequences of Shyness." JOURNAL OF PER-
SONALITY 45 (No. 4): 596-611.

Plomin, Robert, and D. C. Rowe. 1979.
"Genetic and Environmental Etiology of Social Behavior in Infancy."
DEVELOPMENTAL PSYCHOLOGY 15, pp. 62-72.

Rapoport, Judith L. 1989.
THE BOY WHO COULDN'T STOP WASHING. New York: E. P.
Dutton.

Reznick, J. S., et. al. 1987.
"Inhibited and Uninhibited Children: A Follow-Up Study." CHILD
DEVELOPMENT 54, pp. 660-680.

Schachter, Stanley. 1959.
THE PSYCHOLOGY OF AFFILIATION. Standord: Stanford University Press.

Sheehan, David V. 1983.
ANXIETY DISEASE. New York: Charles Scribner & Company.

Sheehan, David V., and J. B. Claycomb. 1984.
"The Use of MAO Inhibitors in Clinical Practice." In Manschreck,

J.C. (Ed.), PSYCHIATRIC MEDICINE UPDATE. New York: Elsevier, pp. 45-60.

Sherif, Muzafer. 1956.
"Experiments in Group Conflict." SCIENTIFIC AMERICAN 195 (November): 54-58.

Sherman, Clay. 1984.
STRESS-FREE LIVING. Chicago: Nightengale-Conant.

Simonton, O. Carl, et. al. 1978.
GETTING WELL AGAIN. Los Angeles: J. B. Tarcher.

Suomi, Stephen J. 1981.
"Inherited and Experimental Factors Associated with Individual Differences in Anxious Behavior Displayed by Rhesus Monkeys." In Klein, Donald F., and J. Rabkin (Eds.), ANXIETY: NEW RESEARCH AND CHANGING CONCEPTS. New York: Raven Press.

Suomi, Stephen J. 1987.
"Genetic and Maternal Contributions to Individual Differences in Rhesus Monkey Biobehavioral Development." In Klein, Donald F. (Ed.), PSYCHOBIOLOGICAL ASPECTS OF BEHAVIORAL DEVELOPMENT. New York: Elsevier.

Thomas, Alexander, and Stella Chess. 1968.
TEMPERAMENT AND BEHAVIORAL DISORDERS IN CHILDREN. New York: New York University Press.

Thomas, Alexander, and Stella Chess. 1970.
"The Origin of Personality." SCIENTIFIC AMERICAN 223 (August): 102-109.

Thomas, Alexander, and Stella Chess. 1982.
"The Reality of Different Temperaments." MERRILL-PALMER QUARTERLY 28, pp. 1-28.

Thomas, William I., and Florian Znaniecki. 1920.
THE POLISH PEASANT IN AMERICA. Chicago: University of Chicago Press.

Walster, Elaine, et. al. 1966.
"Importance of Physical Attractiveness in Dating Behavior." JOURNAL OF PERSONALITY AND SOCIAL PSYCHOLOGY 4 (No. 5): 508-516.

Ward, Ingeborg. 1972.
"Prenatal Stress Feminizes and Demasculinizes the Behavior of Males." SCIENCE 175 #4017 (January): 82-84.

Weintraub, Pamela. 1981.
"The Brain: His and Hers." DISCOVER 2 (April): 15-20.

Wender, Paul H., and Donald F. Klein. 1981.
MIND, MOOD AND MEDICINE. New York: Farrar, Straus, Giroux.

Zimbardo, Philip G. 1961.
"Anxiety, Fear, and Social Affiliation." JOURNAL OF ABNORMAL AND SOCIAL PSYCHOLOGY 62, pp. 356-363.

Zimbardo, Philip G. 1977.
SHYNESS; WHAT IT IS: WHAT TO DO ABOUT IT. Reading, Massachusetts: Addison-Wesley.

Zimbardo, Philip G., and Shirley L. Radl. 1982.
THE SHY CHILD. New York: Doubleday.

Index